T0114507

Albert Murray

The Hero and the Blues

Albert Murray was born in Nokomis, Alabama, in 1916. He grew up in Mobile and was educated at Tuskegee Institute, where he later taught literature and directed the college theater. A retired major in the U.S. Air Force, Murray has been O'Connor Professor of Literature at Colgate University, visiting professor of literature at the University of Massachusetts in Boston, writer-in-residence at Emory University, and Paul Anthony Brick Lecturer at the University of Missouri. His other works include *The Omni-Americans* and *The Hero and the Blues*, collections of essays; *South to a Very Old Place*, an autobiography; *Stomping the Blues*, a history of the blues; *Train Whistle Guitar* and *The Spyglass Tree*, novels; and *Good Morning Blues: The Autobiography of Count Basie* (as told to Albert Murray). His most recent novel is *The Seven League Boots*.

The Hero
and the Blues

Albert Murray

VINTAGE BOOKS

A DIVISION OF RANDOM HOUSE, INC.

NEW YORK

FIRST VINTAGE BOOKS EDITION, JULY 1995

Library of Congress Cataloging-in-Publication Data
Murray, Albert.
The hero and the blues/Albert Murray. — 1st Vintage Books ed.
p. cm.
Originally published: [Columbia] : University of Missouri Press,
[1973], in series: The Paul Anthony Brick lectures.
ISBN-13: 978-0-679-76220-1
1. American literature—Afro-American authors—History and criticism—Theory , etc. 2. Afro-Americans—Songs and music—History and criticism. 3. Blues (Music)—History and criticism.
4. Heroes in literature. I. Title.
PS153.N5M87 1995
810.9'896073—dc20
94-45205
CIP

Contents

The Hero and the Blues

1.

THE SOCIAL FUNCTION
OF THE STORY TELLER

Storybook images are as indispensable to the basic human processes of world comprehension and self definition (and hence personal motivation as well as purposeful group behavior) as are the formulas of physical science or the nomenclature of the social sciences. Such basic insights as may be derived from the make–believe examples of literature are, moreover, as immediately applicable to the most urgent problems of everyday life as are "scientific" solutions.

With this premise, it might not be too much to say that the most delicately wrought short stories and the most elaborately textured novels, along with the most homespun anecdotes, parables, fables, tales, legends, and sagas, are as strongly motivated by immediate educational (which is to say moral and social) objectives as are the most elementary gestures, signs, labels, directives, and manuals of procedure. Indeed, at bottom perhaps even the most radical innovations in rhetoric and in narrative technique are best appreciated when viewed as efforts to refine the writer's unique medium of "instruction." In other words, to make the telling more effective is to make the tale more to the point, more meaningful, and in consequence, if not coincidentally, more useful. Nor

is the painter or the musician any less concerned
than the writer with achieving a telling effect.

Many contemporary American writers, editors,
publishers, reviewers, and, alas, even teachers—and
accordingly an ever increasing proportion of the general American reading public—seem to have forgotten, however, that fiction of its very nature is most
germane and useful not when it restricts itself to
the tactical expediencies of social and political agitation and propaganda as such, but when it performs
the fundamental and universal functions of literature
as a fine art, regardless of its raw material or subject
matter. Moreover, literary "instruction," far from being indirect, is concomitant with artistic purpose as
well as being multidimensional and comprehensive.
As a matter of fact, fiction at its best may well be a
more inclusive intellectual discipline than science or
even philosophy. It can also function as an activating
force which at times may be capable of even greater
range and infinitely more evocative precision than
music.

In truth, it is literature, in the primordial sense,
which establishes the context for social and political
action in the first place. The writer who creates
stories or narrates incidents which embody the essential nature of human existence in his time not
only describes the circumstances of human actuality
and the emotional texture of personal experience,
but also suggests commitments and endeavors which
he assumes will contribute most to man's immediate

welfare as well as to his ultimate fulfillment as a human being.

It is the writer as artist, not the social or political engineer or even the philosopher, who first comes to realize when the time is out of joint. It is he who determines the extent and gravity of the current human predicament, who in effect discovers and describes the hidden elements of destruction, sounds the alarm, and even (in the process of defining "the villain") designates the targets. It is the storyteller working on his own terms as mythmaker (and by implication, as value maker), who defines the conflict, identifies the hero (which is to say the good man—perhaps better, the adequate man), and decides the outcome; and in doing so he not only evokes the image of possibility, but also prefigures the contingencies of a happily balanced humanity and of the Great Good Place.

Thus no matter how sincere his intention, the writer does not automatically increase the social significance and usefulness of his fiction by subordinating his own legitimate esthetic preoccupations to those of the social and political technicians. If he so subserves, he only downgrades the responsibility which he alone has inherited. He discontinues or reduces the indispensable social and political service which art alone can provide, only to do something which many competent journalists (given a functional point of view or doctrine—or a line of jive) can do as well and most good promoters can do

better. Such an action on the part of a writer is every
bit as regressive as that of, say, a surgeon who deserts
the operating room to become a first-aid corpsman
on the battlefield. It is as self-contradictory as the
act of an expert on policies and programming who,
under the illusion of making himself more useful,
resigns a key administrative position to become a
subordinate who grinds out practical campaign slo-
gans in the advertising department of the same or-
ganization. Or, worse still, isn't it indeed much the
same as giving up a position on the coaching staff to
become a cheerleader? What has he done except
leave defining fundamentals in terms of his own
sense of life only to represent somebody else's formulas?

No truly serious or truly dedicated writer can afford to enlist in any movement except on his own
terms. The risks of arrogance which he runs by in-
sisting on such politically suspect individuality are
occupational hazards against which only his integrity
can protect him; and furthermore, every time he
writes any story at all he runs the same risks by pre-
suming that his own conception of heroic action (or
nonheroic action) is significant enough to deserve as
many readers as he hopes will buy or borrow his
books. His discipline no less than his responsibility
is his own in both instances. He must elect to be
consistent with himself and suffer the consequences
—or enjoy them!

Other people can always hold the writer accountable for everything he does, of course; but he can allow no one to tell him what to write. Not even the most expert editorial advisors can do any more than help him execute that which he himself has already conceived and designed. Nor does the social or political technician take over where the writer leaves off. The writer never ceases being concerned with human fulfillment. The programming and activating work of the engineer and technician, on the other hand, is only the means by which fiction becomes fact. Obviously it is the engineer, not the writer, who exercises the workaday authority which translates conceptions into actual social structures and institutions. But even so, in the final analysis it is the writer who determines which social and political systems and functional structures are adequate. Thus even as it was his word, which is to say his conception and image, that was the beginning because it stimulated the vision and aspiration, so is it likely to be his word which signals that end which is also another beginning. What must be remembered is that people live in terms of images which represent the fundamental conceptions embodied in their rituals and myths. In the absence of adequate images they live in terms of such compelling images (and hence rituals and myths) as are abroad at the time. Where there is no adequate vision the people perish, one might say, precisely because where there are no "good" writers there are always "bad" writers, where there are no adequate images there are always inadequate images. Yet the quality of the "serious" art of the times whether adequate or not is likely to be reflected in the popular art of the times.

Nothing else fulfills the inherently consummate intellectual or ideational function of the image-making processes so well as does literature. Not even the most exact and comprehensive scientific information about individual and group impulses, drives, motives, frustrations, repressions, releases, compensations, and sublimations is equivalent to either the personal or the general significance of the writer's singular and indispensable insight into the poetic, dramatic, or mythological dimensions and possibilities of the human situation. Nor for that matter was science in any form ever really intended to be anything more than a functional adjunct and auxiliary to the creative imagination. Technology exists within the context of ritual and myth, not vice versa.

And yet not only do many American writers now proceed as if the social science survey were an adequate extension of fiction, but some obviously assume that personalized journalism geared to the research methodology of the behavioral sciences can actually supersede the creative process in writing. Indeed, there are reviewers, critics, and teachers who suggest even now that fiction is obsolescent and that books which recall experience in terms of the psycho–socio–political–documentary image are already becoming well established as the New Genre which will provide the most adequate frame of reference for coming to terms with contemporary experience.

There are many American readers who now as much as admit that they are uncomfortable with any fictional representation of experience until they have translated each character and gesture and every sequence of action into the terminology of social science. What no writer with serious literary aspirations can afford to overlook, however, is that, far from extending the implications of the traditional categories of tragedy, comedy, and farce, the basic assumptions of contemporary American social science —most of which seem to derive from the formulations or quasi–scientific fabrications of Marx and Freud—only correspond to the oversimplifications of the melodramatic success story. Perhaps such fiction does represent a new genre, social science fiction fiction. The function it performs, however, as necessary as in its limited way it may very well be, is not that of literature but perhaps primarily that of social and political agitation and propaganda.

It was once stated with unmistakable import that only by some "miracle of development" could Ernest Hemingway manage to acquire the "Marxist imagination" of a Leon Trotsky; and Trotsky himself in a review [*] entitled "La Revolution Etranglée" was moved to indict André Malraux for making *The Conquerors* a work of fiction instead of a book of more

---

[*] *Nouvelle Revue Française*, April 1, 1931.

accurate historical documentation. But while it is true that in theory Marxism, like Freudianism, operates on the dynamics of thesis–antithesis–synthesis as does narration, it is also all too true that in actual practice the Marx–Freud imagination of the social science oriented American writer is of its very nature likely to be restricted to the immediate implications of materialistic salvation through psycho–socio–political engineering.

The socio–political or social science fiction fiction hero, who should not be confused with the detective story hero, would achieve salvation by environmental change through revolution, whether by military or legislative measures. But predicated as it is upon scientific programs for remedial action, such a conception never acknowledges the fundamental condition of human life as being a ceaseless struggle for form against chaos, of sense against nonsense. Thus, in spite of temporary plot complications and setbacks, the normal expectation in every social science melodrama is that everything will turn out all right. In fact, last–minute aid for the social science hero can often be assumed to be as available as the nearest telephone!

Not that all social science fiction heroes are successful by any means. Some are defeated precisely because assistance does not arrive in time or at all, or because such assistance as does arrive is inadequate. Others show excellent prospects only to be reduced to invalids by evils within the system as described in statistical surveys. Sometimes the social science fiction hero is a cripple among cripples, all products of systematic oppression, and his only function is to indict the system by displaying his wretchedness! Many Marx–Freud melodramas are specifically designed to demonstrate that the "system," the environment in a social structure, will destroy all mankind if it is not transformed. In any event, it is always the so–called system (political and economic habitat) which generates the complications in the social science plot structure. Thus since the successful social science fiction hero achieves his ends (or at least saves his skin) because he is able to outwit or beat the system, the one who fails does so only because he is deficient in scientific technique (and moral purpose, to be sure). As defined not only by Marxians and Freudians, but also by social reformers in general, all of the essential problems of humanity can either be solved or reduced to insignificance by a hero or man of good will who can apply adequate scientific insight to Public Administration and medicine.

(The assumptions underlying the behavior of the popular contemporary detective story hero are perhaps more consistent with the experience [and resulting perceptions of actuality] from which truly contemporary sensibilities are derived. Such detective story protagonists as Sam Spade, Nero Wolfe and Archie, Phillip Marlowe, and Dick Tracy also symbolize the hero as a scientist, a technician. But in this instance he is primarily a research technician. Sometimes he may take the action necessary to dispatch evil, but his essential job is to dig up evidence and provide information about the source or sources of specific evils. Once he accumulates enough evidence for an "indictment," the detective has, to all intents and purposes, completed the job he was hired to do and may collect his fee and move on to the next client. He provides existential information, not millennial salvation.)

But no writer who restricts his imagination to the assumptions and categories of social science and limits his concern to issues which are essentially political is likely to evolve a genre which fulfills the function of literature. It can be conceded readily enough that in all fiction there is perhaps no more exemplary protagonist than one who, whether he succeeds or fails otherwise, achieves a successful personal integration as a human being while engaged in action to promote the general welfare. But the writer who would create such a hero and would communicate the most immediate as well as the most comprehensive implications of such a view of human behavior must do so in terms of categories, conceptions, and dimensions of human existence which are necessarily beyond the scope and concern of the social sciences. The categories which the story teller requires, and which as an artist he can hardly afford to regard as by–products of non–literary objectives, are those of tragic and comic heroism and farce. The frame of reference within which he works is not that of the scientific research laboratory but that of literature. The dynamics by which he functions are not those of engineering but those of the epic. Indeed, much goes to show that farce, which is in a sense the anticategorical narrative category, is precisely the frame of reference which may be most compatible with the existential absurdity of contemporary actuality.

Science, of course, is an indispensable source of information for the contemporary writer. It is, furthermore, a necessary part of his highly technological environment. Thus it is also an inevitable component of his sensibility and a decisive even if often unapprehended component of his creative imagination. But science is not in itself an elemental wellspring of literature. Promoters of the Genre of the Documentary Image notwithstanding, even the most refined and precise research data are only raw materials which may or may not become literature. For whatever becomes a work of art of any kind does so as a result of an act of creation, an act of esthetic composition, an act involving the art of make–believe. Scientific "statements" or "remarks" as such, even when they are valid, reliable, and comprehensive, are not literature.

Even the unaltered found objects on exhibition in museums of contemporary art are creations. The deliberate act of selection (isolating, highlighting) is a process of transformation not essentially different from choosing, arranging, and giving relative emphasis to scenes and incidents in the composition of a story. After all, the decision to appropriate a given relic, pebble, or mechanical device was not made by a scientist in terms of archaeology, geology, or engineering, but by an artist in terms of esthetic perception.

As for the scientific research document, when it reads like fiction it does so because whoever compiled it possessed dramatic insight and employed the techniques of narrative composition. Realism in literature, after all, is only an esthetic *device,* and it is no less dependent upon craftsmanship than are the devices necessary to the concoction of fantasy. A narrative seems realistic because it was designed (and polished!) to create that effect. An unedited film or tape recording of people acting perfectly naturally is not very likely to create the effect of "slice of life" realism at all. The effect it creates might well be that of tedious unreality. The truth may often be stranger than fiction, but objective documentation is seldom as interesting and effective as skillful dramatic fabrication.

The act of documentation, then, needless to say, is not an act of literary creation. (The pseudo–document is of course a form of fiction, but that is another story.) Documentation is an act which is designed to provide systematic or scientific information. But such information, which is not always reliable but which might well add up to a Documentary Image nevertheless, is useful to the writer of fiction only insofar as it contributes to the credibility of what Susanne K. Langer has called the Dynamic Image, by which she means a perceptible form (such as created by a dance movement) that expresses the nature of human feeling. What the writer, no less than the actor, uses the factual detail and the natural gesture for is to create illusion. A story is a work of the writer's imagination. It seldom follows an actual occurrence with the step–by–step accuracy of the historical record—and even when it does, each step immediately becomes an act in a play which the story teller has contrived from the original events.

THE ABORIGINAL source of fiction, which seems to be the same as that of poetry and drama, is the song and dance ritual or *molpê*. Indeed, the art of fiction may also be regarded as a verbal equivalent to and extension of the art of composition and choreography. The story teller works with language, but even so, he is a song and dance man (a maker of *molpês*) whose fundamental objectives are extensions of those of the bard, the minstrel, and the ballad maker which, incidentally, are also those of the contemporary American blues singer. When he creates short stories and novels, the writer no less than these or the ancient Greek playwrights is composing and choreographing song and dance imitations of experience. It is by means of such imitations that he evokes the dynamic image which embodies and expresses his conception of human nature and of the meaning and purpose of human conduct.

It is also by means of such imitation that literature fulfills its function as a fundamental vehicle of information, instruction, wisdom, and moral guidance. The song and dance ritual, whatever its extensions, whether as drama, lyric poem, ode, hymn, lay, epic, ballad or blues, is not only a reenactment–creation, but also a reenactment illustration, demonstration, and initiation. Even as the short story and the novel embody and thus describe and define the world as the writer perceives it, they also serve to initiate the reader into it. When the writer *relates* a story to the reader, he literally *connects* him with what the story is about. He makes the reader aware of information which establishes a relationship between the reader and the writer's point of view, his scale of values, and his sense of human existence.

Further, the work of fiction, having been created, not only exists as an artifact in the static sense, but also functions as a performance. Each short story and each novel is, that is to say, a dance–extension performance, such as that which the blues singer gives when rendering a ballad for an audience. Thus, when the reader opens a book of fiction, his action is essentially the same as that of entering a theater and opening the curtain or switching on the projector. What he encounters is a production which has been written instead of staged or filmed; what he witnesses as he reads is the entertainment provided by performers in a theatrical fabrication—performers who exist not only to provide entertainment and amusement, however, but who may also provide specific instruction and general education; who show what happens in given circumstances and why it happens, but, perhaps most fascinating of all, how it happens.

The emotional response of the reader to his experience of a book of fiction is also a reenactment (of a reenactment!). Moreover, the dynamics of recall, recognition, repetition, imitation, reconstruction, and recreation involved in such reader–audience reenactment are precisely those which underlie the entire educational process. The interaction of performer and audience is nothing if not that of instructor and student. As he turns page after page, following the fortunes of the storybook hero, the reader is as deeply engaged in the educative process as if he were an apprentice in a workshop. Indeed, he is an apprentice, and his workshop includes the whole range of human possibility and endeavor. His task is to learn from the example of journeymen and master craftsmen such skills as not only will enable him to avoid confusion and destruction, but also will enhance his own existence as well as that of human beings everywhere.

He is, by literal and historical as well as metaphorical extension, a dance apprentice who studies postures, gestures, movements, and positions, each one of which is a statement. The dancer taking a position (and thereby creating a landscape with figures) is also taking a stand, performing a stasimon, creating a stanza, and making a statement of definition. Making a gesture and executing a step, he is also taking action which is based on an established position or point of departure, and on a definition of circumstance, situation, and predicament. At the same time he is also taking an action which creates another situation which requires another definition which suggests further action!

The apprentice who has sufficient aptitude becomes a journeyman and eventually a master craftsman. All educational systems, formal and informal alike, seem to operate on some principle of graduation, the final stage of which is a commencement of independent individual application of the skills, knowledge, awarenesses, appreciations, and attitudes, etc. The master craftsman in any trade is, appropriately enough, one who knows the tread, which is to say the tracks which make the course or the way, the route and routine, the way to and the way to do. He is, that is to say, an erstwhile apprentice and journeyman who can execute the most intricate steps in an outstanding manner.

No master craftsman ever really learns everything about his line of endeavor, of course. Even at best his applications are still only a form of practice. He is a practician and follows his trade. The exceptional degree of expertise which he does develop, however, not only qualifies him to function on his own, but also enables him to extemporize under pressure and in the most complicated circumstances. Nor is a higher degree of erudition and skill possible, or even relevant. Improvisation, after all, is the ultimate skill. The master craftsman is one for whom knowledge and technique have become that with which he not only performs but also plays (one performs a dance as one plays music, and when one plays in a drama one is performing in a play). The master craftsman is also one who, as the hero in combat and the blues musician in a jam session, can maintain the dancer's grace under the pressure of all tempos.

The song and dance rituals which underlie tragedy, comedy, melodrama, and farce—the four standard categories of narrative literature, all extensions of the epic—not only provide conclusive evidence of the fiction writer's inherent and inescapable involvement with measures which contribute to human welfare; they also reveal the functional value of such involvement. When the writer's aspirations are truly literary, his dedication to the art of fiction is tantamount to a social commitment to human well–being and self–realization. His sense of art is inseparable from his sense of what is beneficial and what is detrimental in human existence.

When he writes in terms of the story pattern known as tragedy, for instance—which is in effect the retracing of the steps leading to destruction and which, as the name suggests, may well be the extension of the goat sacrifice song and dance or the Dance of the Scapegoat—he is performing a purification ritual in imitation of the life process itself. Indeed, according to Gilbert Murray, in *The Classical Tradition in Poetry,* "Tragedy is the enactment of the death of the Year–Spirit; and comedy is the enactment of his marriage, or rather of the Comos which accompanies his marriage. The centre of tragedy is death; the centre of comedy is a union of lovers."

Gilbert Murray then goes on as follows:

Thus Greek drama starts, not as a mere picture of ordinary life, or even of ordinary adventure, but as a re–creation, or *mimesis,* of the two most intense experiences that life affords; a re–creation of life at its highest power. The purpose of the drama was—it is generally agreed—originally magical. The marriage Comos was intended actually to produce fertility; the death–celebration was the expulsion of evil from the community, the casting out of the Old Year with its burden of decay, of the polluted, the Scapegoat, the Sin–Bearer. It is well to remember that dramatic performances were introduced into Rome in order to cure a pestilence. This occurred actually during the lifetime of Aristotle. But Aristotle himself has forgotten as completely as we have that tragedy was ever a magical rite: he treats it simply as an artistic performance, and judges it, not for any concrete effect it may have on the public health, but simply on aesthetic grounds. And this shows us that, for whatever reason it was created, drama persisted and increased because it answered to some constant need in human nature.

Several paragraphs later Murray also claims that tragedy "hides or adorns the coming 'bulk of death,' magnifies the glory of courage, the power of endurance, the splendor of self–sacrifice and self–forgetfulness, so as to make us feel, at least for the fleeting moment, that nothing is here for tears, and that death is conquered."

Perhaps the "happy ending" that is commonly associated with the story pattern of comedy does not so much suggest that death has been conquered as that life has been mastered, at least for the moment and at least to an extent which will allow for human continuity. The implications of the symbolic reenactment of the union of lovers as represented in the boy–meets–girl, boy–loses–girl, boy–gets–girl formula, for example, go beyond survival through copulation as such. Coming as it does after the hero has made his way through certain tribulations, the happy ending is in effect a most fundamental statement about the nature of security. As a direct result of his adventures it can be assumed that the hero has acquired enough practical first–hand experience to handle a passable amount of such difficulties as are inherent in the nature of things. The lessons he has learned are the very essence of security, which is to say survival. Perhaps another way of suggesting what is essentially the same thing is that the hero does not get the girl until his experience indicates that he is somewhat better prepared to assume the responsibilities of parenthood. In any case, the embrace which so often represents the happy ending is not the prelude to retirement. The happy ending, precisely like a marriage, is only the end of courtship. It is the beginning of family life—and so forth and so on!

The melodrama or adventure story, a typical climax of which is also the union of lovers, may well have been derived from rituals of purification as well as fertility. In fact, it is a story in which the union (or atonement) of lovers is predicated upon purification. But unlike the tragic hero whose problem is his own contamination (his own flaws, mistakes, choices, or whatever), or the comic hero whose problem is his naïveté, or lack of perception, the melodramatic hero of some sagas, of some medieval romances, and of the scientific success story purifies society. He overcomes his inadequacies, which are mostly technological, by following the proper instructions and acquires the magic formula which cures and saves an ailing body politic.

There are also elements of ritual purification and fruitful union in that category of narration known as farce. Indeed, the writer can transform any tragedy, comedy, or melodrama into a farce simply by changing his rhetorical tone and manner. A performer need make only the slightest change in his gestures in order to turn an act of purification into slapstick, the union of lovers into an obscene frolic, and heroic behavior into the ludicrous gesticulations and misadventures of a Don Quixote. When the actor, the dancer, or a writer like Cervantes does so, however, what he creates is perhaps not simply a subspecies of tragedy, melodrama, or even comedy, but in a sense another ritual altogether. What he actually accomplishes even when his intentions are satirical is the disintegration of tragic, comic, and melodramatic forms along with all other ideas of purposeful order, including the notion of common sense—which becomes stuff and nonsense.

Essentially, a farce, which always involves subversive intrusion, is a capricious or goat–like song and dance symbolizing disorder. As such it is a ritual reenactment not of goat sacrifice or of sacred totemic copulation but rather of the absurd and outrageous and inexorable resurgence of nature itself. It is thus in the most elemental sense a mock ritual which functions as a counter–agent of ritual. In a farce it is as if the intended scapegoat were revolting and desecrating the purification ceremony. It is as if the goat–footed bridegroom were turning the wedding procession into a feast of lasciviousness. Farce breaks the spell of ritual. It counterbalances the magic which ritual works upon the imagination. It protects human existence from the excesses of the imagination and operates as a safeguard against the overextension of ideas, formulations, and formalities. After all, extended far enough, even the idea of freedom becomes a matter involving security measures and thus a justification for restrictions which exceed those that generated the thrust toward liberation in the first place. The world is, or should be, all too familiar with totalitarian systems which began as freedom movements.

In ultimate effect, farce is a divine, Olympian, or cosmic joke, and as such it is an indispensable antidote for the wisdom of the ages. It is, that is to say, the ridiculous prank without which no formal occasion can be viewed in proper perspective, for as ironic as it may seem, frivolity and sensual intemperance exercise a *moderating* influence on the holiness of holiday sacraments—even now, when the word holiday has become a synonym for debauchery.

On the other hand, the absurd and outrageous intrusion of nature–in–the–raw is also that which all heroes must confront. Such is the fate and mission of every hero in every situation, whether he is the protagonist in a Greek drama, in a medieval romance, or in an American blues ballad; he must recognize that which threatens human existence and must either withstand and subdue it or be annihilated by it. In the end, of course, it is always raw nature itself, the unconscious and irresponsible, inexorable earth in all its natural chaos which abides. Nevertheless, the hero whose aspirations are always those of Prometheus, but whose very seriousness makes him resemble Don Quixote, presumes, endeavors, and somehow succeeds even when he fails.

At bottom every hero is, like a solo dancer on an

empty and infinite stage, always the protagonist in
an epic. He is, that is to say, the representative man
who pits himself against nature in the raw (which
of course is also nature–in–the–absurd, thus making
him also a buffoon in a farce, a minstrel clown cut-
ting capers which somehow coordinate, a whiteface
or blackface fool whose outlandish and silly statements somehow make sense out of its nonsense). In
all events it is always some destructive or anti–
human element in nature against which the hero
contends, whether his immediate circumstances be
those of tragedy, comedy, melodrama, or farce. In
the typical tragedy, for instance, it is nature itself or
the nature of things which generates the plot—
which entraps the hero. The tragic hero, as defined
here then, is actually an epic hero who falls victim
to the atrocities which are inherent in the nature of
things.

The comic hero thus becomes an epic protagonist
whose difficulties are also inherent in the very nature of actuality. He mistakes, misinterprets, and
misconstrues appearances and is misled into pande-
monium, from which he narrowly extricates himself
only because he begins to see things for what they
actually are and can proceed not in spite of but in
terms of (in the specific terms of) complexity. His
story line: on his way to perform the act of union
which will fructify all mankind, the comic hero, perhaps because he thinks good offices are enough, is
led astray. But as a result of the adventures which

follow, when he finally does make it to the sacred grove where the fertility rites are performed, he has learned enough to realize that sweet smiles and words and beautiful weather and landscapes can lend to confusion as well as happiness.

The comic situation is based on the fact that nature, or rather man's perception of it, is forever jumping out of focus. At some point in perhaps most melodramas, however, it pops back into focus, revealing a configuration of itself which is all too sharp and unmistakable. What the hero must enjoin in combat at that point, depending upon whether the story is an epic–like saga, a romance, a gothic adventure tale, a chronicle of crime and detection, or a dime novel, is a monster, usually from the depths of a pond, a swamp, or the world ocean; a dragon from the infernal bowels of the earth, a weird beast from the wilderness; or it may be and perhaps most often is a villain, a person that is to say of.lowest estate, one from the most nature–like regions, from the outer edges of civilization, an outlaw from the regions beyond law and order, a gangster from the underworld. The smoothie in the penny dreadful cliff hanger is another aspect of the same narrative convention. In the end he always reveals himself to be the rawest and most brutal elements of nature in disguise. Beneath all the highly polished veneer of elegance and pretty manners which in retrospect were somewhat suspicious or at least disconcerting all along, is a senseless but murderous selfishness which makes him an all but unmistakable personification of the heartlessness, soullessness, and mindlessness of natural forces (*which in the context of farce become the invisible "blue devils" that beset the nimble-or-nothing hero at every turn*).

Thus do such esthetic considerations as types of narrative statement involve such ethical matters as categories of heroic action; and thus is the story teller's moral obligation or social commitment inherent in his craft. The art of fiction is an art of make–believe. It is therefore, and precisely by the same token, also an art of persuasion and even of propaganda. But what the story teller in his capacity as artist wants those who respond to the fortunes of the storybook hero to believe goes far beyond the credibility of any given political formulation. Even when specific political issues motivate the plot he is recounting, the story teller's point is still that of the fable underlying all drama: Once upon a time there was someone who somehow did or did not achieve that favorable, no matter how delicate, balance between essential human values on the one hand and cosmic absurdity (as well as political outrage) on the other.

2.

THE DYNAMICS OF HEROIC ACTION

The remark which Ernest Hemingway made in *Green Hills of Africa* about writers being forged in injustice has two very functional implications which are of immediate relevance to writers—black and white—who would use the experience of black people in the United States as material for fiction. The first is obvious: Hemingway was convinced that the experience of such things as war, upheaval, poverty, and injustice were not of themselves bad for writers. On the contrary, he felt that such experience, as horrible as it is for mankind at large, could actually be of great advantage for writers. In his opinion Tolstoy, Dostoevsky, Stendhal, and Flaubert, for instance, were all better writers for having been involved in human life at the elemental level of wartime existence, revolution, exile, and so on.

Such experience, Hemingway knew only too well, involves disenchantment and alienation; but he also knew that it tests the writer's basic values, improves his perspective and objectivity. He spoke of the necessary shock to cut the "overflow of words." In "Monologue to the Maestro" he tells a young apprentice that the best early training for a writer is an unhappy childhood; and in *A Moveable Feast* he re-

membered his days of poverty in Paris as being good
for his discipline. In replying to George Plimpton's
question about writing and injustice (in an inter-
view for *Paris Review*), he went on to say that the
most essential thing for a good writer was a built-in,
shockproof crap detector, which (he told Robert
Manning, then of *Time* magazine in another inter-
view) should have a manual drill and crank handle
in case the machine breaks down.

The first implication of Hemingway's remark about
justice thus becomes obvious as soon as one realizes
that all serious writers have had a deep-seated sense
of exclusion, disaffection, alienation, disillusionment,
detachment, dissatisfaction, disorientation, and so
on, and that this as much as anything is what makes
them tick as writers.

The second implication is not so obvious at first
glance. Its significance, however, extends beyond
the writing process as such and into the dynamics
of the blues tradition as a whole. In a sense the
whole point of the blues idiom lyric is to state the
facts of life. Not unlike ancient tragedy, it would
have the people for whom it is composed and performed confront, acknowledge, and proceed in spite
of, and even in terms of, the ugliness and meanness
inherent in the human condition. It is thus a device
for making the best of a bad situation.

Not by rendering capitulation tolerable, however,
and certainly not by consoling those who would com-
promise their integrity, but—in its orientation to

continuity in the face of adversity and absurdity—
the blues idiom lyric is entirely consistent with the
folklore and wisdom underlying the rugged endurance of the black American. In addition, or rather
concomitantly, blues–idiom dance music challenges
and affirms his personal equilibrium, sustains his humanity, and enables him to maintain his higher aspirations in spite of the fact that human existence is
so often mostly a low–down dirty shame.

Hemingway himself, it should be understood, did
not spell out any elaborate theory of cultural dynamics in this or in any other connection. Nor is
there any evidence that he ever concerned himself
to any great degree with comprehensive intellectual
formulations as such. His intellectual discipline was
the craft of fiction, and most of his nonfiction was
either his special brand of personal journalism or observations which suggested practical everyday guidance for writers; and, far from thinking of any of
his suggestions as the principles which in truth they
are, he was much more likely to claim only that they
worked for him. The excuse which he gave for pub-
lishing "Monologue to the Maestro," for example,
was that some of the information it contained would
have been worth the price of a copy of *Esquire*
Magazine to him when he was twenty–one.

Nevertheless, the image of the sword being forged
is inseparable from the dynamics of antagonistic cooperation, a concept which is indispensable to any
fundamental definition of heroic action, in fiction or

otherwise. The fire in the forging process, like the dragon which the hero must always encounter, is of its very nature antagonistic, but it is also cooperative at the same time. For all its violence, it does not destroy the metal which becomes the sword. It functions precisely to strengthen and prepare it to hold its battle edge, even as the all but withering firedrake prepares the questing hero for subsequent trials and adventures. The function of the hammer and the anvil is to beat the sword into shape even as the most vicious challengers no less than the most cooperatively rugged sparring mates jab, clinch, and punch potential prize-fighters into championship condition.

Heroism, which like the sword is nothing if not steadfast, is measured in terms of the stress and strain it can endure and the magnitude and complexity of the obstacles it overcomes. Thus difficulties and vicissitudes which beset the potential hero on all sides not only threaten his existence and jeopardize his prospects; they also, by bringing out the best in him, serve his purpose. They make it possible for him to make something of himself. Such is the nature of every confrontation in the context of heroic action.

It is all very ironic, of course, but after all experience itself is not only ironic, it is sometimes downright absurd. Science, whether physical or social, cannot abide irony and absurdity, but there is nothing it can do about them. On the other hand, all great story tellers have always known that irony and absurdity are not only thorns in the briarpatch in which they themselves were bred and born but also precisely what literary statement is forever trying to provide adequate terms for!

Which is a very good reason indeed why promising young men in stories, as in life, do not become heroes by simply keeping their police records clean and their grade point averages high enough to qualify them for status jobs and good addresses inside the castle walls. Nice young men are the salt of society, the soul of respectability, the backbone of the nation, and their faces appear at court functions and their names are recorded on official documents. But those young men who become the heroes whose deeds merit statues, red–letter days, and epics do so by confronting and slaying dragons.

Moreover, the outlying regions, the sinister circumstances beyond statistics, *cooperate* with the hero by virtue of the very fact of and nature of their existence. They help beget real–life and storybook heroes alike, not only by generating the necessity for heroism in the first place but also by contesting its development at every stage and by furnishing the occasion for its fulfillment. Indeed, since in the final analysis the greatness of the hero can be measured only in scale with the mischief, malaise, or menace he can dispatch, the degree of cooperation is always equal to the amount of antagonism.

Everyday manifestations of this kind of cooperation are infinite. Complicated diseases, for example, wreak havoc, but they also bring out the best doctors and the best in doctors. Without exasperating legal snarls there are only ordinary inexperienced lawyers, however promising. Schools with the most difficult course requirements turn out the best trained graduates. Strict factory testing procedures guarantee dependable products. And so it goes. Nor should there be any confusion because of the elimination involved. What brings out the best also shows up the worst, a procedure as indispensable as it is paradoxical.

Much has been made of the inevitability of fate in ancient Greek mythology. But as much, if not more, can be made of the dynamics of antithesis. Greek drama has as much to do with perception through purpose and passion as with predetermination; Greek tragedy, as is well known, was concerned with catharsis, which was always the result of confrontation and struggle, and as such it was a testing, elimination, forging and proving process, designed to achieve a durable synthesis, whether of personal fibre or of common sense.

Sometimes, as in the story of Oedipus, the cooperative antagonist is all too conspicuous by his absence. All Oedipus wants is to be a nice fellow and avoid trouble, and yet his very best deeds only serve to bring him closer to the disaster he is running away from. A young man of obvious if somewhat naïve good intentions, Oedipus is not actually undone by the oracle which predicts that he will murder his father and marry his mother, but by his unwillingness to stay in Corinth and face his problems. In some ways it is as if Oedipus were essentially a social science–oriented intellectual (born centuries before the contemporary vogue) whose basic assumption is that life can be free of ambivalence, complexity, and strife. He proceeds as if there were actually environments antiseptically free from folly and safe against sin—welfare states, as it were, moderately taxed but well budgeted against social problems and therefore immune to personal conflicts.

Whatever his assumptions, his first–hand knowledge of human complexity is inadequate, and he oversimplifies his circumstances in terms of his own good intentions. But his integrity, which has not been forged in "cooperative" injustice but in loving courtly care, is not rugged enough to withstand the provocations and temptations of everyday life. Thus he is noble enough not to want to harm his father but not actually generous enough to defer to a cantankerous old stranger at the crossroads. High IQ undergrad type that he is, he can answer such academic questions as are put by Ivy League sphinxes, but he is not really hip enough to realize that he should never make love to any queen under any circumstances. He hastens to call in the experts and survey technicians to find out what is wrong with other people but never suspects that anything might be wrong with himself. He never even tries to find out why he has been walking with a limp all of his life (which incidentally, also means he doesn't even know the *meaning* of his name, which actually summarizes his biography). He is, in this, somewhat like the white American who seems unable to realize that it is the oppressor not the oppressed, whose condition is inherently and intrinsically pathological. The oppressed, after all, is faced with very real threats and hostilities outside himself. Anxiety, and even terror, are intrinsically normal responses to danger.

Oedipus, who in a sense really has no mission except to avoid trouble, begins his journey untried in the ways of mischief. Shakespeare's Prince Hal, on the other hand, becomes a worthy King Henry V because he has served an apprenticeship in the regions outlying the castle and has become wise in the ways of Falstaff and his ruffians.

THE BULLFIGHT, which never ceased to fascinate Hemingway, is a ritual in which the element of antagonistic cooperation is more clear–cut and fundamental. By definition the good fighting bull is a cooperative antagonist to the extent that he provides the dangers (i.e. opportunities for risk taking) without which there can be no good matadors and therefore no *corridas* worthy of the name. In the bullfighter, Hemingway studied at close range a very special exemplification of the hero in action. Not only is the matador a volunteer who seeks out, confronts, and dispatches that which is deadly; he is also an adventurer who runs risks, takes chances, and exposes himself with such graceful disdain for his own limitations and safety that the tenacity of his courage is indistinguishable from the beauty of his personal style and manner.

Such a conception of heroism is romantic, to be sure, but after all, given the range of possibilities in human nature and conduct, so is the notion of the nobility of man. And so inevitably, whether obvious or not, are the fundamental assumptions underlying every character, situation, gesture, and story line in literature. For without the completely romantic presuppositions behind such elemental values as honor, pride, love, freedom, integrity, human fulfillment, and the like, there can be no truly meaningful definition either of tragedy or of comedy. Nor without such *idealistic* preconceptions can there be anything to be *realistic* about, to protest about, or even to be cynical about.

The unbelievably splendid conduct of the bullfighter has the same basic ritualistic function as the superhuman exploits and escapades of the epic protagonist. It affirms that which is upstanding in human nature, that which stands out against the overwhelming odds of the nonhuman and anti–human elements in the universe. The bullfighter, like the epic hero, is the beau ideal, the prototype and paradigm of the positive potential in all human behavior, and most noteworthy of all, he inspires the ordinary man, the individual, to extend himself beyond routine conceptions and achievements.

AMERICAN protest fiction of the current Marx/ Freud–oriented variety is essentially anti–adventure and, in effect, nonheroic. It is predicated upon assumptions which have much more to do with philanthropy than with the dynamics of antagonistic cooperation. It concerns itself not with the ironies and ambiguities of self–improvement and self–extension, not with the evaluation of the individual as protagonist, but rather with representing a world of collective victims whose survival and betterment depend not upon self–determination but upon a change of heart in their antagonists, who thereupon will cease being villains and become patrons of social welfare! It is as if such writers see human experiences in terms of melodramatic predicaments, only to substitute supplication for precisely that heroism which Marx/Freud–oriented surveys and ideologies would seem to require, for revolutions are nothing if not adventures.

Heroism, which is, among other things, another word for self–reliance, is not only the indispensable prerequisite for productive citizenship in an open society; it is also that without which no individual or community can remain free. Moreover, as no one interested in either the objectives of democratic institutions or the image of democratic man can ever afford to forget, the concept of free enterprise has as much to do with adventurous speculations and improvisations in general as with the swashbuckling economics of, say, the Robber Barons.

There may be ever so much passion and bloodshed in protest fiction. But since its blackest rage and most sanguinary confrontations are likely more often than not to be designed primarily as indictments against indifference, injustice, or brutality, rather than as examples of the obstacles which beset all quests for manhood, or rather personhood, selfhood, the just society, and everything else, such fiction belongs not to the literature that provides images which, to paraphrase André Malraux, enable men to become aware of the greatness in themselves that they might otherwise ignore. It belongs to the rhetorical category of supplication.

In effect, protest or finger–pointing fiction such as *Uncle Tom's Children* and *Native Son* addresses itself to the humanity of the dragon in the very process of depicting him as a fire–snorting monster: "Shame on you, Sir Dragon," it says in effect, "be a nice man and a good citizen." (Or is it, "Have mercy, Massa?") Indeed, in their fiction no less than in their essays, writers like Richard Wright, James Baldwin, and their imitators often seem to be appealing to the *godliness* of the dragon: "O, you who are so all powerful, let my people go." When you name the dragon the devil, as Malcolm X used to do, or pig, as Eldridge Cleaver does now, aren't you really trying to convert him by putting the bad mouth on him?

Nor is the threat a heroic weapon.

Why is it that so few moral outcry protest agitators seem to realize or even to suspect that all political establishments are always likely to have built–in devices to counteract the guilt and bad conscience which the exercise of power of its very nature entails? Aren't political establishments or administrations likely to function much the same as some U.S. business establishments that have special departments to handle complaints, while the other transactions flow on as usual?—the ever so nice smiles in the complaint department making up for the defective goods in the stockroom!

Sometimes, to be sure, a power establishment does respond with corrective action, or at least some show of corrective action. But many times it responds with crestfallen acknowledgment and little else, compensating for its crime by feeling genuinely sorry for the victim. At other times it may simply allow the discontents to blow off hot air until their sense of frustration is relieved enough or they become bored enough with themselves to settle back down into the routine. And so on it goes. Nobody was probably ever more obscenely naïve and self–defeating than certain ever so wrathful moral outcry militants who do not realize which of their accusations and threats are effective and which are simply being indulged, and who don't even seem to suspect that sometimes indulgence is all they are going to get for their efforts.

But then, contrary to any fundamental commitment to heroic action, protest fiction seems to assume that the risks involved in such action should be avoided, averted by massive official action. Over any romantic implications of shining armor the protest writer seems to prefer the humility of sackcloth and ashes. Instead of the man on horseback, it seems content to promote the man of moderation and peace —or the loud-mouthed wretch who hurls abuse at those whom he quite obviously assumes to be his betters, who stations himself and his picket-troops at some safe and convenient capital city wailing wall and beseeches or browbeats the partly deaf Olympians of the Power Structure to send official decontamination squads into his boondocks to spray the dragons away. Even when the outraged protest writer threatens damnation, it is easy for anybody to see that he is mostly only bluffing and that the real threat is in the confusion being propagated. Most dragons are well aware of the fact that when his threats materialize as violence, the protest writer is likely to be as surprised and confused as everybody else, that what he really wanted to do all along was negotiate for legislation and appropriations. Most Northern-style U.S. dragons are not at all unmindful of how easy it is to get some of the loudest protestors to settle for a few compassionate reassurances that some one is beginning to Give a Damn.

Not that anyone in his right mind should or would ever hesitate to seek and use all available tax–supported anti–dragon forces—or refuse to take every possible preventive measure. Nevertheless, it is hardly wise to proceed as if any nation or community will never need any more citizen dragon fighters who are battle–seasoned in hand–to–hand combat. For not only must there always be someone qualified to command the official anti–dragon operations, but there also must be adequate forces in being and in reserve to be mobilized and deployed.

Without such forces prayer availeth naught and the threat of damnation even less. And yet the estimates of the situation upon which most American protest fiction is based would seem to indicate that any effective resistance is impossible, except by people whose fitness is evidently based on the fact that they have never had to resist anything. Almost every gesture in recent American protest fiction seems designed to convince the reader of one thing above everything else: Dragons bring only terror and devastation. But if this is so, then the writers of protest fiction can only be agents of sheer nonsense. They are professional supplicants who are in the grotesquely pathetic position of making urgent requests which they cannot possibly believe will be honored by the enemy. And how can they believe that their threats of rebellion and revolution can be fulfilled by their dragon–withered fellow victims of the Wasteland? As any basic training NCO will tell you, it will take forever to make effective combat troops out of the sad sacks in all those statistical surveys.

On the other hand, the writer who deals with the experience of oppression in terms of the dynamics of antagonistic cooperation works in a context which includes the whole range of human motivation and possibility. Not only does such a writer regard anti–black racism, for instance, as an American–born dragon which should be destroyed, but he also regards it as something which, no matter how devastatingly sinister, can and will be destroyed because its very existence generates both the necessity and the possibility of heroic deliverance. The firedrake is an evocation to the hero, even as the very existence of dangerous big game animals was in itself a call to Hemingway's huntsmen.

The fiction writer whose imagination is essentially philanthropic, whether its orientation is to the benevolent foundations, liberal politics, Marx/Freud–utopianism, or welfare–state ideology, is likely to regard the protagonist not as an image of man the giant killer, but as the personification of a cause in need of benefactors. Such a protagonist, of course, is no hero at all. He is the underdog, and far from projecting charisma, he evokes compassion. He is an object not of inspiration, but of sympathy and even of pity.

Any storybook hero worthy of his name, however, is more often than not an object of admiration or emulation. Even when he fails, there is something in his deportment that inspires others to keep trying. Even his difficulties are considered desirable. Indeed, as every schoolboy should remember easily enough, to aspire to heroism is to wish for the adventures of Ulysses, the obstacles of Hercules, the encounters of Sir Lancelot—and so on, to the predicament of Hamlet or the poverty and isolation of Stephen Dedalus.

The implications for contemporary American writers, whether black or white, should be easy enough to grasp: Precisely as white musicians who work in the blues idiom have been simulating the tribulations of U.S. Negroes for years in order to emulate such musical heroes as Louis Armstrong, Lester Young, and Duke Ellington, and such heroines as Bessie Smith and Billie Holliday, so in fiction must readers, through their desire to imitate and emulate black storybook heroes, come to identify themselves with the disjunctures as well as the continuities of black experience as if to the idiom born. Moreover, the basis for such omni–American fiction is already in existence. Even now young white activists are beginning to regard themselves and their problems, with however much imprecision, in terms which are largely black. In any case, it may already be somewhat easier for them to project themselves as black civil rights activists than to imagine themselves as ancient Greek Argonauts, or even as early modern British seadogs and nineteenth–century Empire builders, not to mention the Indian fighters and slave traders that some of their own American ancestors actually were—*and not so very long ago either.*

THOMAS MANN, whose essay *The Coming Victory of Democracy* is one of the most compelling statements of the case for commitment in contemporary literature, once thought of himself as being a nonpolitical man. When the consummate craftsman and Olympian ironist who wrote *The Magic Mountain, Joseph and His Brothers,* and *Doctor Faustus* was an incredibly gifted younger man writing *Buddenbrooks, Tonio Kroger,* and *Death in Venice* (any one of which would qualify him as a contemporary master), he regarded art as being of its very nature separate from such everyday concerns of life as politics. Art in the bourgeois Germany of his youth, he later confessed, was assumed to exist in the very special domain of culture, which to him included music, metaphysics, psychology, a pessimistic ethic, and an individualistic idealism, and from which he "contemptuously excluded everything political."

Such assumptions did not reduce the validity of his early fiction, however, for, significantly, even as he proceeded in terms of a conception based on what he was later to regard as an artificial separation of art from life, he was preoccupied with the theme of the personal, social, and human incompleteness of the truly dedicated artist—who accepts his isolation in the Ivory Tower but also yearns for the simple and "normal" life, "the blisses of the com monplace." Mann, whose insight into the relationships between genius and pathology, between creativity and criminality, was characteristic of his distinctive and definitive irony, never overromanticized the role of the artist in society.

Nevertheless, in his longest work of nonfiction, *The Reflections of a Non-Political Man*, he insisted on the necessity for the artist to remain aloof from politics. At this time he defined democracy as the political functioning of the intellect, and he immediately rejected such functioning as a threat to culture and even to freedom. But what he meant by freedom then was moral freedom, and of the connection between moral freedom and social freedom he "understood little and cared less."

But when he came to write the foreword to *Order of the Day*, he could look back on his *Reflections* as the extended prologue to a long series of manifestoes and attestations. The book itself, he says in the essay "Culture and Politics," has been the expression of a crisis, in response to profoundly disturbing events which had caused him to examine the question of the individual human being and the problem of humanity as a whole as never before, and he came to see that there is no clear dividing line between the intellectual and the political, that the German bourgeoisie had erred in thinking that a man of culture could remain unpolitical.

He also came to realize that culture itself stood in

the greatest danger wherever and whenever it lacked interest and aptitude for the political. The nonpolitical man had equated democracy with the readiness of the intellect to be political only to condemn it. But not only did the free world spokesman recommend it in *The Coming Victory of Democracy*, he had also come to equate political behavior with human behavior. The self–exiled, world–renowned man of letters, writing "Culture and Politics" in the United States at a time when totalitarian forces had completely enslaved his homeland, could only thank his "good genius" that the anti–political inhibitions of his German upbringing had not suppressed the "feeling for democracy" which followed *The Reflections of a Non–Political Man.* "For where should I stand today," he wrote, "on what side should I be if in my conservatism I had clung to a Germany which in the end had not been saved by all its music and all its intellectualism from surrender to the lowest form of worship of power, nor from a barbarism which threatens the foundations of our Western Civilization."

The political essays and speeches in *Order of the Day* repudiate the restricted conception of the writer as artist which *The Reflections of a Non–Political Man* represented. But the effect which *Mario and the Magician, The Magic Mountain, Joseph and His Brothers,* and *Doctor Faustus* had on the earlier fiction was that of enrichment. In retrospect, the line of development from Tonio Kroger,

the gifted ambivalent outsider, through Hans Cas
torp, the competent, ambivalent engineer, to Joseph,
the fantastically endowed if still somewhat ambivalent provider, seems not only natural but irrepressi-
ble. In progress, however, it had all of the complexities involved in the dynamics of thesis, antithesis,
and synthesis (complexities which only reinforce its
consistency).

The antithetical crisis during which Thomas Mann
progressed from esthetic isolation to social consciousness and commitment was The War and After-
math. His response to the world–shattering events
which began with the outbreak of war in 1914 led
first to the defensive introspection of *The Reflections*, and then to the revelation of democracy and
the realization of the nature of his involvement in
mankind—and to his subsequent metamorphosis,
not only into a Humanist but also into the epic poet
and prophet of what he called The Coming, The
New, or The Third Humanism.

The Magic Mountain, the narrative of Hans Castorp's seven–year sojourn among the living dead in
the nether world of a sanitorium in the Swiss Alps,
was published in 1924 and was, in addition to its
other dimensions, Mann's testament of the Apoca-
lypse. It was also his Book of the Transfiguration.
Thus it is as if Mann's output through *Death in
Venice* were deliberately designed to describe an
antecedent state of error (or of erroneous innocence)
while that which begins with *The Magic Mountain*

is both the process and the embodiment of the New Enlightenment.

The introverted adventures of Hans Castorp provide adequate evidence of the difficulties involved in the self–induced metamorphosis which Mann undertook as a writer and underwent as a man. They also reveal the very special nature of the transfiguration achieved: he did not become a new man; he became a new extension of the old man, or rather, of the young man. So thoroughgoing was the self–reexamination that the result, ironically, was not so much an eradication and replacement as a synthesis. The new creature was very much the product of the old. There is much of Tonio Kroger the Artist in Joseph the Provider. Tonio has not been destroyed; he has been modified by new elements and by a more comprehensive re–combination. Incidentally, the nature of such recombination is given playful but no less profound treatment in *The Transposed Heads,* a finger exercise.

The enlistment of Thomas Mann was not a response to the pressures of recruitment. There were such pressures, of course. His situation was, in fact, not at all unlike that of Hans Castorp, who was beset at every turn by the enticements of Settembrini, Krowkowski, Hofrat Berens, and even Claudia Chauchat and Mynheer Peeperkorn. But what Mann reacted to was the totality of his situation; thus the social conscience which he developed was consistent with the actual complexity of human nature. What

Mann enlisted to serve was therefore not a political
doctrine such as Marxism but a new conception of
man in which political involvement is inseparable
from cultural security.

What he called the New Humanism or the Third
Humanism was both consistent and comprehensive.
It did not flatter man by looking at him through
rose–colored glasses. It was based on a hard–headed
awareness of man's dark, demonic "natural" side as
well as a reverence for his suprabiological spiritual
worth. The new humanity would also be universal;
"and it will have the artist's attitude; that is, it will
recognize that the immense value and beauty of the
human being lies precisely in the fact that he belongs to the two kingdoms of nature and spirit. It
will realize that no romantic conflict or dualism is
inherent in the fact but rather a fruitful and engaging combination of determinism and free choice,
upon that it will base a love for humanity in which
its pessimism and its optimism will cancel each
other."

The New Humanism is at the core of everything
Mann wrote from *The Magic Mountain* onward. But
nowhere does it achieve a more comprehensive formulation than in the special dimensions of the image
of Joseph, the hero of *Joseph and His Brothers*. It is
Joseph, the seer and provider, with his fabulous
fusion of poetic imagination and political skill, who
is best equipped of all Mann's protagonists to confront and come to realistic terms with the problems

of contemporary existence. No epic hero is without flaws, of course: there is Joseph's sometimes unmanageable egoism, and, among other things, there is (or was for a long time) also his extremely peculiar and, in truth, not altogether masculine involvement with flirting, of teasing others to the point of seduction while regarding his own chastity as sacred. But he is as well prepared as any other hero in modern fiction to function in the circumstances of the world described by André Malraux; furthermore, he is equipped (perhaps precisely by his egoism and compulsion to flirt with danger) to assume the responsibilities (or risks) of leadership in such a world.

It is easy enough to project Joseph forward into the revolutionary China of *Man's Fate* or into the beleaguered Spain of *Man's Hope*. But it is also, if anything, even easier to resurrect him as an immigrant to the contemporary United States (which on balance might well be an infinitely more complicated milieu than was Egypt during the time of the Pharaohs). Nor is it insignificant that Thomas Mann himself had become an immigrant to the United States when he wrote the episodes which define the Provider. But perhaps even more significant evidence of Joseph's contemporary immediacy is the altogether fascinating fact that the seemingly undauntable optimism which supports his flexibility no less than his tenacity of purpose makes him an excellent epic prototype for the U.S. Negro hero—who, like him, it should be remembered, was also sold into bondage.

Indeed, Afro Americans will find that Joseph shares fundamental qualities in common with the epic hero of the blues tradition, that uniquely American context of antagonistic cooperation. Joseph goes beyond his failures in the very blues singing process of acknowledging them and admitting to himself how bad conditions are. Thus his heroic optimism is based on aspiration informed by the facts of life. It is also geared to his knowledge of strategy and his skill with such tools and weapons as happen to be available. These are the qualities which enable him to turn his misfortunes into natural benefits. At any rate, he proceeds as if each setback were really a recoil action for a greater leap forward, as if each downfall were a deliberately designed crouch for a higher elevation.

Perhaps Joseph's physical endowments are not as impressively athletic as those required for a U.S. Negro protagonist. But then the Negro hero should not be confused with the heavyweight champion of the world, either. As a matter of fact, Jack Johnson, the greatest of all heavyweight champions, fought with the agility of a middleweight. Mann makes it clear enough that the golden brown Joseph is neither too tall nor too short, but precisely the right height —which is as it should be. After all, no hero was ever as huge and as powerful as a dragon. Moreover, heroic achievements are a matter of supernatural skill, not extraordinary brawn. Indeed, it is entirely possible that heroes are tall, for instance, only in the imagination of those who need them—for in action, even the six–foot–six gladiator is a darling, beleaguered underling. In any case, the actual physical appearance of even the greatest of heroes, for all their charisma, is frequently so unimposingly average that special effort seems nooooooary in order to set them apart from the proverbial man in the street. It is as if the typical hero has to be borne on the shoulders of worshipful admirers, bedecked with special raiments, elevated to special platforms, and thence to thrones and ultimately to pedestals in order that he may look impressive enough to be capable of the miraculous feats of championship which he has in fact already accomplished. In all events his relatively unprepossessing physical stature only intensifies the hero's glamour and mystery, even as it humanizes and universalizes his appeal.

Nevertheless, Joseph, unlike the U.S. hero in general and the U.S. Negro hero in particular, does not exhibit any special physical dexterity and prowess along with his incomparable spiritual tenacity. Not that any hero, even Hercules, ever had as much physical strength as moral courage. Perhaps also, in spite of all his smooth talk and tantalizing ways, Joseph may strike most U.S. Blacks as being somewhat deficient in sensual gusto, if not sophistication. He is, alas, for all his good looks, not really a very extraordinary man among women. Indeed, not unlike the naïve Oedipus who compounds his troubles by making love to the wrong woman, Joseph, by attracting and then refusing the wrong one, is brought to the very brink of disaster, from which he escapes only because his errors always have a way of turning out to be blessings in disguise.

But even so, there is good reason to assume that given the necessity, Joseph, who is not only an irresistible sweet man and a first-rate stylist withal, but also a most apt desegregationist indeed, could put together the prerequisite combination of patent-leather finesse, rawhide flexibility and blue steel endurance to swing, tip, or stomp with uptown authenticity at the Savoy and in other situations as well. Nor should it be forgotten that Joseph's conduct is oriented to both choice and chance.

It is no more difficult to project the Joseph of Thomas Mann into the blues tradition than it could possibly have been to get Moses from the Old Testament into the spirituals—and, religious objectives aside, there is good reason to believe that it might be an even more rewarding undertaking. For while Negroes have been overlooking the special implications of Joseph's journey into Egypt, they have been overemphasizing the role of Moses as Messiah and grossly oversimplifying what the Exodus was really all about. Many have been teaching, preaching, singing, and signifying about Moses and the Promised Land for generations without ever making any practical or political application of the obvious fact that in U.S. terms, being half this, half that, he was a mulatto! Nor do they seem to have found anything significant in his role as lawgiver and utopian; and they seem completely oblivious to the confusion inherent in identifying with a nationalist who defines freedom and fulfillment in terms of leading his people out of the country of their actual birth and back across the sea to some exclusive territory.

Joseph, on the other hand, not only uses his inner resources and the means at hand to take advantage of the most unlikely opportunities to succeed in the circumstances in which he finds himself; he also makes himself indispensable to the welfare of the nation as a whole. Those who follow Moses are forever talking about going back home; but to Joseph, to whom being at home was as much a matter of the spirit as of real estate, anywhere he is can become the Land of Great Promise.

No one can deny to Moses, great emancipator that he was, the position as epic hero of anti–slavery movements. But neither should anyone overlook what Joseph, the riff–style improviser, did to slavery. He transcended it to such an extent that his previous "condition of servitude" became the sort of apocryphal cottonpatch–to–capital–city detail so typical of U.S. biography. Only a Horatio Alger could look at the elegantly tonsured and tailored Joseph at a function of state and believe that such a fine figure of a man was once not only a slave but a convict. As for Joseph himself, he never regarded himself as being anything other than a Prince of the Earth. He never, even in the deepest and foulest dungeons, thought of

himself as an outcast, but rather, as Mann points out
time and again, he saw himself as *a man set aside
for a special purpose.*

The Joseph which Thomas Mann has created in
Joseph and His Brothers represents the human being
as artist and improviser. The emphasis which in the
fiction of Ernest Hemingway is always placed on the
skill and style of the hero is another way of making
what is essentially the same literary statement. And
what André Malraux declares to be the function of
art indicates just how fundamental such a "statement" is. All art, he says in *The Voices of Silence*
(as elsewhere), is a revolt against man's fate, against
the limitations of human life itself. And the victory
of each individual artist over his servitude imple-
ments the eternal victory of art over the human situation.

Not that Thomas Mann requires very much cor-
roboration in such matters. *The Magic Mountain,*
after all, is the story of the transformation of an engineer into a man who has begun to master the art
of living! When Mann refers to the mundane Hans
Castorp as life's delicate child or the problem child
of nature, he is obviously associating and perhaps
deliberately confusing Castorp's ordinary burgher
sensitivity with the esthetic sensibility of an artist
like Tonio Kroger. Man, he points out in *The Coming Victory of Democracy,* is not only a part of nature, he is also the means by which nature becomes
aware of itself. Thus the erstwhile seemingly robust

but now admittedly fragile Hans Castorp, taking stock of himself while recuperating in a sanitorium, personifies nature become conscious of itself, developing a conscience—and acquiring a sense of responsibility. Hence the obligations of heroism.

In *Order of the Day*, Mann refers to art as man's guide on the difficult path toward understanding himself. "Art is hope," he writes in the statement defining humanism, but which has no less to do with the storyteller's preoccupation with the dynamics of heroism. "I do not assert that hope for the future of mankind rests upon her shoulders; rather that she is the expression of all human hope, the image and pattern of all happily balanced humanity."

3.

THE BLUES AND THE FABLE
IN THE FLESH

André Malraux defines art as the means by which
the raw material of human experience becomes style.
He contends that stylization, whether abstract or
representational, is the supreme objective of the
creative process. He also maintains that the artist
derives not from nature itself but from other artists
and that the sense of life which any given artist expresses always involves an interaction with other
works of art. "Never do we find an epoch–making
form built up without a struggle with another form,"
he states and reiterates throughout *The Voices of
Silence;* "not one problem of the artist's vision but is
conditioned by the past." Nor does there seem as
yet to be any evidence from either archaeology or
anthropology to refute him. "Always," he writes in
reference to existing examples of prehistoric art such
as the rock paintings of Rhodesia and the cave paintings of Altimire and Lascaux, "however far we travel
back in time, we surmise other forms behind the
forms which captivate us." As for the modern folk or
modern primitive art, he points out that for all their
apparent crudeness, innocence, and assumed naturalness, such forms likewise follow conventions and
traditions which it would be rash to ascribe to

naïveté alone. The painters at our country fairs," he adds as a reminder, "know well what subjects are expected of them . . . and what styles these call for."

Applied to the art of fiction, Malraux's description of the dynamics of artistic creation suggests a practical point of departure which is both consistent with the history and geography of contemporary man and also commensurate with the complexity of contemporary experience and esthetic sensibility. Along with Malraux's conception of the museum without walls, which may well have been derived from long existing anthologies of world literature in the first place, this description also provides a working context within which the contemporary writer can come to practical terms with what is perhaps the most fundamental issue underlying every problem of craftsmanship involved in the actual process of literary composition: the functional relevance of literary tradition to the immediate requirements of vernacular communication.

T. S. Eliot addressed himself to what he defined as the problem of tradition and the individual talent and concluded that it was necessary for the writer to live in what is not merely the present but the present moment of the past. Tradition, he held, as did Thomas Mann in his essay "Freud and the Future," is not something dead but rather that which is already living. In Eliot's sense as in Malraux's, tradition is thus as much a part of the writer's environment as anything else. "The historical sense," Eliot insisted, "compels a man to write not merely with his own generation in his bones but with a feeling that the whole of the literature of Europe from Homer and within it the whole of the literature of his own country has a simultaneous existence and composes a simultaneous order." The historical sense, which he goes on to describe as a sense of the timeless and the temporal together, is what makes a writer traditional, *but it is also what makes him* "most acutely conscious of his place in time, of his own contemporaneity."

The manner in which Eliot employed specific elements from medieval romance and ancient ritual along with fragments from literary works in *The Waste Land,* however, seems to have been as misleading to some as it has been instructive to others. Not unlike the many who were confused by James Joyce's use of ancient Greek mythology in *Ulysses,* there are those who ignore the actual style and texture of the poem and mistake as the total statement what is essentially only the point of departure. The revelation of a traditional mythological substructure of human existence is not the objective of Eliot's poem. Nor did Joyce write his novel on the assumption that the art of fiction was really a matter of pigeonholing contemporary characters and events in terms of prototypes in antiquity.

Ulysses is not a contemporary adaptation of the *Odyssey,* only an allusion to it—an arrangement, which is to say a contemporary orchestration based on the chordal structure and progression of the *Odyssey*. The creative process for Joyce, as for Eliot, was a matter of making the most of the inevitable interaction of tradition and the individual talent. He used his scholarly insights not to discover and certainly not to establish mythological parallels and equivalencies for Irish experience, but to enrich his poetic imagination. In *Ulysses* he created his own local mythological system, the "cosmic" framework of which is one day in Dublin. (Essentially the elements of classical myth in *Ulysses*, like those in *The Waste Land*, are used as historical puns—or perhaps one might even call them mnemonic devices.) What is really of most immediate significance about Molly Bloom, for instance, is not that she is the reincarnation (or modernization) of a figure or figures from classical mythology and primitive ritual (which she is of course), but that in her Joyce created a compelling image in a mythological romance of his own. Anna Livia Plurabelle in *Finnegans Wake* also echoes other voices from many other times, towns, and villages, but she herself is nothing if not a mythological figure of contemporary Ireland. She is James Joyce's Irish conception and creation of an Irish woman. She is his Irish image of all women, not simply his Irish repetition of other images in other stories. She is his complex and richly informed (but no less Irish for being universal) metaphor to represent the Irish female to end all females, his Irish womb of the world, as it were, the vernacular Irish female to end and begin again and again all males as well as females.

Joyce began (as Malraux claims all artists do) by imitating existing models, which, thanks to the printing press, represented a range as wide as all of the content in accessible libraries. Much has been made of the international essence of *The Portrait of the Artist as a Young Man, Ulysses,* and *Finnegans Wake.* But what the contemporary apprentice must also remember is that James Joyce, who has become for so many students of literature an archetype of the twentieth century literary cosmopolitan, always wrote out of a sensibility that became more and more sophisticated about the world at large only to become more and more Irish at the same time, even as it embraced the idea of timelessness in order to remain up to date.

Ernest Hemingway, who was no less cosmopolitan and no less sophisticated in the use which he made of tradition than were Eliot, Joyce, Malraux, or even Thomas Mann, was especially concerned about the misuse of it. The remarks he made to express his longstanding misgivings about being able to distinguish what one actually experiences from what one has been taught to respond to represent a fundamental and comprehensive protestation against the misapplication of traditional meanings. So was his reference to Thomas Wolfe's overflow of words. But on a number of occasions he also focused his attention on the problem of the writer's specific relationship to tradition as such. At one juncture in *Green Hills of Africa*, for instance, he mentions Poe as being a skillful writer, Melville as being good sometimes in spite of the rhetoric; and then he goes on to register a protest, the implications of which are temporal as well as geographical and environmental. "There are others," he points out, "who write like English colonials from an England of which they were never a part to a newer England that they were making very good men with the small, dried and excellent wisdom of Unitarians; men of letters; Quakers with a sense of humor."

He was referring to "Emerson, Hawthorne, Whittier and company. All our early classics who did not know that a new classic does not bear any resemblance to the classics that have preceded it. It can steal from anything that it is better than, anything that is not a classic, all classics do that . . . But it cannot derive from or resemble a previous classic. Also these men were gentlemen or wished to be. They were all very respectable. They did not use the words that people always have used in speech, the words that survive in language. Nor would you gather that they had bodies. They had minds, yes. Nice, dry, clean minds . . . ."

His own accent was unmistakably contemporary and unquestionably American. And yet *The Sun Also Rises*, for instance, can be read in the same timeless, international mythological–ritualistic frame of reference as *The Waste Land*. It is as accurate to refer to Jake Barnes as being a Fisher King as to say that he is an impotent expatriate. On the other hand, when he is placed in the mythological context which underlies *Ulysses*, Jake the war veteran takes on overtones of a marooned Odysseus—perhaps (but not necessarily) on the Isle of Circe. But in the end as in the beginning, just as *Ulysses* is a story about an Irishman in Dublin, so is *The Sun Also Rises* a story about an American in Paris (and Spain). So rich is the natural heritage of the writer today that such multilevels can be the resonance of a truly contemporary voice.

ESSENTIALLY, questions about experimentation in the arts are also questions about the relevance of tradition. They are questions, that is to say, about the practical application of traditional elements to contemporary problem situations. Hence they are also questions about change and continuity. Indeed, they are specifically concerned with the requirements for continuation, which is to say endurance, which also is to say survival. Implicitly, experimentation is also an action taken to insure that nothing endures which is not workable; as such, far from being anti–traditional, as is often assumed, it actually serves the best interests of tradition, which, after all, is that which continues in the first place. The traditional element is precisely the one which has endured or survived from situation to situation from generation to generation. To refer to the blues idiom is to refer to an established mode, an existing context or frame of reference.

But then not only is tradition that which continues; it is also the medium by which and through which continuation occurs. It is, or so it seems in the arts at any rate, precisely that in terms of which the objectives of experimentation are defined, and against which experimental achievements are evaluated. Accordingly it is within the tradition of fiction that innovations in fiction evolve—and no matter how startling such innovations turn out to be, their effect is not to destroy fiction but to enhance and *extend* it. Perhaps a better word for experimentation as it actually functions in the arts is improvisation. In any case, it is for the writer, as for the musician in a jam session, that informal trial and error process by means of which tradition adapts itself to change, or renews itself through change. It is, that is to say, the means by which the true and tested in the traditional regenerates itself in the vernacular.

The more any art form changes, by whatever means and by whatever methods, motivations, or infusions, the more it should be able to fulfill its original function. The observations of Suzanne K. Langer on the nature and purpose of art are hardly those of a reactionary. On the contrary, such books as *Philosophy in a New Key, Feeling and Form,* and *Problems of Art,* like Malraux's *The Voices of Silence* and

The Metamorphosis of the Gods, and Hemingway's *Death in the Afternoon* and *Green Hills of Africa,* not only provide a comprehensive justification for experimentation in the arts but also establish a solid point of departure for it.

"Each art," Suzanne Langer writes in *Problems of Art,* in a passage which seems as applicable to fiction as to any other form, "begets a special dimension of experience that is a special kind of image of reality." She refers to this special dimension as "the primary illusion or primary apparition" and states that the arts are defined by their primary apparition and not by materials and techniques. "Painted sculpture is not a joint product of sculpture and painting at all, for what is created is sculpture, not a picture. Paint is used, but used for creating sculpture—not for painting. The fact that poetry involves sound, the normal material of music, is not what makes it comparable to music—where it is comparable."

As for obvious differences which do develop as a result of experimentation, they frequently represent extensions and refinements, but seldom do they represent fundamental changes. The difference between a simple footlog across a stream and that elaborately engineered structure of steel and concrete spanning the Hudson River does not alter the original function of a bridge at all. Perhaps (some American automobile designers notwithstanding) the original functions are more easily obscured in the arts than in engineering, but even so, sooner or later the writer will realize that even those novels which are written to show that there is no story to tell must nevertheless narrate *that* story both effectively and affectively.

New forms do evolve, of course, even as the novel may be an extension of a form which was once known as the *molpê* in Ancient Greece, and by other names elsewhere. But a novelist who creates poems or case histories is no longer a novelist. He has become a poet or a social scientist. A painter using materials and methods of photography is still a painter as long as what he is making is a painting. If what he produces is a photograph with elements of a painting, however, he has become a photographer. In its original military sense, the avant garde is an exploratory extension of the main body of troops. In the arts its advanced position has never been so much a matter of programming as of effect. It is the applicability of his technical achievement which establishes a writer as a forerunner, a pathfinder, and a trailblazer, not his intentions alone, and certainly not the fact that he engages in experimentation as such. In point of fact, inasmuch as the very act of literary creation is always a matter of trial and error, literary composition is in itself an experimental process. Writers are always trying to solve problems of rhetoric, form, style, and so on, through modifications, innovations, and inventions. Experimentation is as indispensable to the development of the individual style of Flaubert and Henry James as to the overall or definitive style of a generation or of an epoch.

The objective of artistic experimentation, whether in the case of the individual or of an entire aesthetic school or movement, is to develop a device with which to render the subtleties of contemporary sensibility. The maximum communication of these subtleties, however, is achieved only to the extent that rhetorical innovations become a part of the natural mode of expression of the time. The lasting results of avant–garde experimentation always become inevitable–seeming parts of the grand style of the mainstream of discourse.

Perhaps every masterpiece represents the assimilation of the grand or epoch–making style (which should not be confused with grand manner or with high style). The grand style is, one might say, the comprehensive rhetorical strategy. It is, in other words, that combination of literary tactics and devices which best enables the writer to encompass or to capture the essential nature, the essential feeling of the experience of his time, place, and circumstances. It is that stylization of experience which actually comes to seem the least stylized. Maurice Grosser, the author of *The Painter's Eye,* makes an observation about the grand style in painting which is directly applicable to fiction. "These people, in Hogarth, in Reynolds, in Goya, in Copley are real," he writes. "And that is the Grand Style, for the Grand Style is no style at all. It is not a way of painting. It is only the painter's greatest subject. It is what every painter strives to paint. It is the painter's view of ultimate reality."

Whenever he was asked about the experimental aspects of his work, William Faulkner invariably answered that he was trying primarily to write about people, that he was simply trying to get the story told by one means or another. Nevertheless, *The Sound and the Fury, As I Lay Dying, Light in August, Absalom, Absalom,* and *The Bear* belong among the most outstanding technical experiments in contemporary American fiction. Nor was Faulkner's experimentation as offhand as his remarks on the subject may suggest. Perhaps he did remain unconscious of much of the natural traditional influence of such writers as Balzac, Mark Twain, Melville, and possibly Henry James (whom, incidentally, he called a prig). But his awareness of the immediate functional implications of both content and technical innovations by such contemporaries as Sherwood Anderson, Joyce, Proust, and even Hemingway for his own work is unmistakable.

Nor, on balance, does he seem to have intended his remarks to be misleading; for there is much to indicate that he was not so much concerned about deprecating or disavowing his involvement with technical explorations as with keeping it in proper perspective. But perhaps his remarks were misleading in spite of all the obvious evidence in the works themselves. In any case, during the time when most of his best fiction was being published he was largely ignored by critics except for supercilious references to his southern subject matter and his compositional obscurity, both of which were regarded as Gothic, decadent, and even degenerate.

Ernest Hemingway, on the other hand (not unlike, say, Louis Armstrong in the world of music), was spotted and celebrated as a significant stylist by critics and writers alike at the very outset of his career. Indeed, the influence of certain aspects of Hemingway's technique is one of the most obvious characteristics of U.S. fiction since the nineteen twenties. Even as Armstrong's influence is evident in U.S. music from the same time forward, most contemporary readers seem to feel that description, dialogue, and narrative pace are most natural when rendered with Hemingway's functional directness. Fiction editors still celebrate the greatness of Herman Melville and Henry James, but they tend to scrutinize manuscripts through Hemingway's reading glasses, true to his influence even as the pop-ballad singers who seem most natural to contemporary American ears are likely to be those who derived (whether directly or indirectly) from Louis Armstrong.

Hemingway himself, however, was no more involved with avant-garde programs *per se* than was Faulkner. The young apprentice in *A Moveable Feast* was working out his own individual problems of craft, as was the student of bullfighting. "In writing for the newspaper," he recalled in *Death in the Afternoon*, "you told what happened and, with one trick or another, you communicated the emotion aided by the element of timeliness which gives a certain emotion to any account of something that has happened that day; but the real thing, the sequence of motion and fact which made the emotion and which would be valid in a year or ten years, or, with luck and if you stated it purely enough, always, was beyond me and I was working very hard to try to get it . . . ."

He was trying to work out his own individual problem, but his response to a *Time Magazine* inquiry about the status of his personal influence in 1947 reveals his insight into the interrelationship of individual accomplishments, tradition, and continuity in one telegraphic sentence: "Hemingway influence," he replied seriously and quite objectively but not without levity, "is only a certain clarification of the language which is now in the public domain."

Nor did he mean simplification; precision, he meant, to be sure, but the clarification he was always working for was multi–dimensional. "If I could have made this enough of a book," he began in the epilogue to *Death in the Afternoon*, "it would have had everything in it." Perhaps the five Hemingway dimensions are as elusive as the figure in the carpet of Henry James, but the out–chorus rhetoric of *Death in the Afternoon* has qualities of fiction, poetry, documentation, and exposition, as well as painting and musical composition. Incidentally, he always listed painters among those from whom he learned how scenes are made, and he also included musicians among his literary forebears. Assuming, as he told George Plimpton, that what he had learned from them would be obvious, also obvious is the fact that he was trying to write fiction, not change its function.

When Faulkner was asked whether there was a conscious parallel between *As I Lay Dying* and *The Scarlet Letter,* his answer was still another revelation of the fact that his working knowledge of the dynamics of literary tradition and the comprehensive nature of the grand style was essentially the same as Hemingway's. "No," he said, "a writer don't have to consciously parallel because he robs and steals from everything he ever wrote or read or saw." He was simply writing a tour de force, and as every writer does, he took whatever he needed wherever he could find it, without any compunction and with no sense of violating any ethics or hurting anyone's feelings "because any writer feels that anyone after him is perfectly welcome to take any trick he has learned or any plot he has used. Of course we don't know just who Hawthorne took his from. Which he did—because there are so few plots to write about."

Faulkner made these remarks at the University of Virginia in 1957. Hemingway, it will be remembered, made his statement about writers stealing from other books (and the one about some writers being born only to help another writer write one sentence) in *Green Hills of Africa* in 1935. Both Hemingway and Faulkner were forever disclaiming any status as intellectuals or men of letters. Culture, Hemingway once declared, with as much insight as irreverence, was a good thing to have, like a 1/1000 map to maneuver on; Faulkner said it was all right, "but to me—I ain't interested in it." "Most writers are not literary men," he said, "they are craftsmen," and elsewhere he referred to writing his books as being "a matter of the carpenter trying to find the hammer or the axe that he thinks will do the best job."

The practical working point of all of this should be clear enough. Ernest Hemingway and William Faulkner, who on balance must be regarded as the most effective twentieth–century American avant–garde fiction writers to date, operated on essentially the same assumptions about the interreaction of tradition and the individual creative talent as did T. S. Eliot and Thomas Mann. Experimentation for them was not an effort to escape or reject the past but a confrontation of the present, or, as Eliot and Mann would have it, the present moment of the past. So far as Hemingway was concerned, all art was created by individuals. When the great individual artist arrives, he "uses everything that has been discovered or known about his art up to that point, being able to accept or reject in a time so short it seems that knowledge was born with him . . . and then the great artist goes beyond what has been done or known and makes something of his own." Even as Shakespeare once did in literature. Even as Duke Ellington has done in contemporary American music.

Indeed, the most valid aspiration as well as the most urgent necessity for any writer who truly takes the social, which is to say the ethical, function of fiction seriously is not to create something at least different if not new but rather to achieve something natural to himself and to his sense of life, namely a stylization adequate to the complexity of the experience of his time and place—and perhaps with the luck of past masters, something that is more than merely adequate. Thus does the writer make his unique and indispensable contribution to good conduct: not by creating a pop–image that illustrates what is only a "conventional" conception of a Revolutionary hero, but rather by projecting an image of man (and of human possibility) that is *intrinsically* revolutionary. Such an image is likely to be automatically at radical odds with the status quo.

ALL OF WHICH has more than a little to do with the literary implications of the dynamics (or natural history) of blues idiom statement *per se:* when André Malraux suggests that art should give man a sense of human grandeur, he expresses a point of view with which perhaps even the most gung–ho of activists would readily agree. But Malraux (himself a veritable prototype of the cause–oriented twentieth century writer) is also fully aware of what art not only involves but requires. "It is a revealing fact," he states in *The Voices of Silence*, "that when explaining how his vocation came to him, every great artist traces it back to the emotion he experienced at his contact with some specific work of art; a writer to the reading of a poem or novel (or perhaps a visit to the theatre); a musician to a concert he attended; a painter to a painting he once saw. Never do we hear of a man who, out of the blue, so to speak, feels a compulsion to express some scene or startling incident . . . What makes the artist is that in his youth he was more deeply moved by his visual experience of works of art than by that of the things they represent . . . ." In other words, the origin for art is likely to be art itself.

The primary subject matter of *The Voices of Silence* is painting and sculpture. But perhaps the observations which Malraux makes about what is in effect the natural history of the creative impulse may also be applied with equal force to musicians who work in the blues idiom. "Artists," Malraux goes on to say, "do not stem from their childhood, but from their conflict with the achievements of their predecessors; not from their own formless world, but from the struggle with the form which others have imposed on life. In their youth, Michelangelo, El Greco and Rembrandt imitated; so did Raphael, Velasquez and Goya; Delacroix, Manet and Cezanne—the list is endless. Whenever we have records enabling us to trace the origins of a painter's, a sculptor's, any artist's vocation, we trace it not to a sudden uprush of emotion (suddenly given form) but to the vision, the passionate emotion, or the serenity of another artist."

Similarly, though few students of American culture seem aware of it, but as those who are truly interested in promoting "black consciousness" in literature should note, what makes a blues idiom musician is not the ability to express *raw* emotion with primitive directness, as is so often implied, but rather the mastery of elements of esthetics peculiar to U.S. Negro music. Blues musicians do not derive directly from the personal, social, and political circumstances of their lives as black people in the United States. They derive most directly from styles of other musicians who play the blues and who were infinitely more interested in evoking or simulating raw emotion than in releasing it—and whose *"primitiveness"* is to be found not so much in the *directness* of their expression as in their pronounced emphasis on stylization. In art both agony and ecstasy are matters of stylization.

Currently popular social science conditioned interpretations notwithstanding, U.S. Negro singers, for example, are influenced far more directly and decisively by Bessie Smith and Louis Armstrong, among others, and by the sonorities of various down-home church rituals than by any actual personal experience of racial oppression, no matter how traumatic. Indeed, what is most characteristic of the black American life style is infinitely more closely related to an orientation to African–derived dance and work rhythms and to the rich variety of music which Afro–Americans have heard in the United States than to any collective reaction to the experiences of slavery and segregation as such.

The actual working procedures of such blues–oriented arrangers, composers, and conductors as those who provided the scores for the orchestras of Fletcher Henderson, Chick Webb, Earl Hines, Jimmie Lunceford, Count Basie, Lionel Hampton, and numerous others can hardly be explained by references to oppression or even economic exploitation. When viewed in the context of artistic creation, however, such procedures can be as immediately understood and as fully appreciated as those of the playmakers who supplied the scripts for the Elizabethan stage companies.

As a matter of fact, the Elizabethan playmaker suggests an historical frame of reference within which Duke Ellington, the most masterful of all blues idiom arranger–composers, becomes the embodiment of the contemporary artist at work. The Ellington orchestra is frequently booked for recitals in the great concert halls of the world, much the same as if it were a fifteen–piece innovation of the symphony orchestra—which in a sense it is. Nevertheless, by original design and by typical employment as well, Ellington's is still an itinerant song and dance band. Moreover, its repertory clearly reflects the fact that over the years most of its performances have been in night clubs, theaters, dance halls, and at popular music festivals. However, it is largely because of, not in spite of, such show business affiliations that the image Ellington the artist so closely resembles is that of the Elizabethan playmaker, whose productions, it must not be forgotten, also began as popular entertainment. Show business motivation underlies Ellington's construction of numbers for the special solo talents of, say, Cootie Williams, Johnny Hodges, and Ben Webster, no more nor less than it underlies Shakespeare's composition of soliloquies for the actor Burbage. This similarity is perhaps at least as important to an understanding of Ellington's esthetics as are existing psycho–political theories about black experience, by which is usually meant black misery.

But what is perhaps even more significant is that the arranger–composer, whose sense of structure and movement is in large measure derived from the small informal combo and the jam session, proceeds in terms of a tradition of improvisation which is fundamentally the same as that which Elizabethans inherited from the *commedia dell' arte*. And when, as often happens, the arranger–composer works from existing tunes as the typical Elizabethan playmaker often employed existing story lines (and as Greek dramatists made use of existing myths and legend), improvisation becomes in actuality the same process of stylization in terms of which Malraux defines all art.

When Ellington creates blues–extension concertos in which the solo instrument states, asserts, alleges, quests, requests, or only implies, while the trumpets in the background sometimes mock and sometimes concur as the "woodwinds" moan or groan in the agony and ecstasy of sensual ambivalence and the trombones chant concurrence or signify misgivings and even suspicions (which are as likely to be bawdy as plaintive) with the rhythm section attesting and affirming, he is quite obviously engaged in a process of transforming the raw experience of American Negroes into what Malraux calls style. He is also stylizing his sense of the actual texture of all human existence not only in the United States or even the contemporary world at large, but also in all places throughout the ages.

Such is the nature, as well as the scope, authority, and implications of art. And it should be just as obvious that Ellington, who is not only a genius but who after all is no less dedicated to music (and no less accomplished at it) than a Herman Melville, a Mark Twain, or even a Henry James was to fiction, is likewise no less involved with what T. S. Eliot referred to as the "objective correlative" or the "objective equivalent" to feeling. Also obvious is that he is concerned (as Suzanne K. Langer in *Problems of Art* points out that all artists are concerned) with the *life of human feeling* (which is to say, how it feels to be human) beyond everything else.

But what should be, if anything, most immediately obvious of all is that for Duke Ellington himself and for the members of his orchestra, textures of human feeling exist in music in terms of arrangements and compositions which are always related to other arrangements and compositions. Accordingly, the performance of an Ellington composition is not nearly so dependent upon the personal feelings of his musicians as upon their attitude toward music and styles of other musicians. The performer's personal feelings do count for something, of course, but only insofar as he can relate them to his musical imagination and his musical technique. The feelings which incompetent arrangements and inept performances seem most likely to involve are confusion, annoyance, boredom and, mercifully, indifference.

Sooner or later those who are truly interested in the promotion of black consciousness or of a black dimension in American literature are likely to discover that "black esthetics," as the saying goes, is not as some agitprop rhetoricians seem to think, simply a matter of a group of spokesmen getting together and *deciding* and then prescribing how black experience is to be translated into poetry, drama, fiction and painting, but rather of *realizing what any raw material of any experience must undergo in order to become art.* How do you give esthetic articulation to the everyday facts of life? The problem of every writer is how to make his personal sense of experience part of the artistic tradition of mankind at large.

In other words, esthetic problems are not likely to require less esthetic insight and orientation simply because the subject matter at hand happens to be black experience. Certainly no artist can accept the suggestion that art is artless. Not even the most spontaneous–seeming folk expression is artless. No matter how crude some folk music, for example, might sound to the uninitiated, its very existence depends on a highly *conventionalized* form. Folk airs, ditties, tunes and ballads are labeled traditional precisely because they conform to well–established even if unwritten principles of composition and formal structure peculiar to a given genre or idiom which, after all, is an esthetic *system* in every essential or functional meaning of the phrase.

As for the currently popular extensions of the old downhome church–derived dance music which pop singers like James Brown, the late Otis Redding, Aretha Franklin, and Ray Charles, among others, express with such "soulful naturalness" not only is such music derived directly from other musicians (many of whom play in downhome style churches), it also undergoes countless very strictly controlled rehearsals. And it is constantly being revised and refined to suit the ear of the arranger–conductor, a process which, by the way, is likely to have as much to do with keeping it "roughed up," natural, and "authentic" as with diluting it. Sooner or later those who would serve their "commitment" through fiction must realize that every masterpiece in literature, as in painting and music, is testimony to the fact that at least as much esthetic technique is required in order to "tell it like it is" as to tell it "like it ain't." The truth may well be even more difficult to relate than it is to find.

In any case, straining for political relevance is likely to produce the same deleterious effect on the creative process as straining for commercial relevance. As most students of art history will perhaps agree, chauvinism is often only another form of the cheapest kind of commercialism.

Such is the nature of art that the only thing the creative person is justified in straining for is his personal point of view, and paradoxically this probably has much to do not with straining but with learning to relax so as to discover how one actually feels about things.

Of course, the fact that so many self–styled *engagé* writers are so impatient to score political points is quite understandable. But the danger is that such well–intentioned impatience may cause writers to neglect precisely those elements of their chosen métier that would enable them to provide the most effective esthetic basis for political statement.

There is, in other words, good reason to assume that whatever his social intentions, the writer is likely to achieve his best (and most useful) work when his mastery of his craft is such that he is able to play with his story, even as the musician plays a score, even as actors play a script, even as athletes play a game.

IN GENERAL, contemporary American writers seem to regard the epic with misgivings as strong as those which Ernest Hemingway expressed in *Death in the Afternoon* when he referred to it as something which bad writers were in love with. Perhaps some contemporary apprehension is a reaction to a "false epic quality" in books such as some of those by John Dos Passos and Thomas Wolfe. Perhaps some is related to those grandiose movie productions, each with a super–colossal cast of thousands, which are also called epics by the writers of Hollywood promotion copy. But perhaps there are also those who have come to realize, as Hemingway no doubt did, that the epic is not nearly so much a matter of intention, deliberation, and design as of comprehensive literary achievement—that stories which have become national epics, like those which have become academic classics, have done so by virtue of the nature of the response they have generated.

In any case, there is not very much evidence in contemporary fiction of any widespread preoccupation with what used to be called The Great American Novel. What the overwhelming majority of contemporary U.S. writers seem to be primarily concerned with instead, however, is The Image of the Individual. The list of American stories about the condition of the individual in the modern world is endless. Furthermore, even those writers who work in terms of the Documentary Image are primarily engaged in bringing the Individual into focus. Nobody expresses more concern about the problems of individual welfare than do writers who are oriented to the social sciences; and of course all political agitation and propaganda in the United States, that of Communists and Socialists no less than of the advocates of free enterprise, begin and end in the name of individual freedom and personal fulfillment.

But all the epic ever required was one individual in the first place. It was never contingent upon wide-screen panoramas, multitudes, or even large-scale actions. Only its implications need be comprehensive —and perhaps even they need less basis than do statistical projections. Moreover, every hero in every story is nothing if not a symbolic individual, and as such he is the Representative Man in the statistical as well as the ritualistic sense. Indeed, Kenneth Burke has suggested that the word *symbolic* may be equated with the word *statistical!* Nor can the statistician deny that his norms are intended to represent the typical.

The storybook hero, of course, is that projection or extension of the typical individual which functions, at least to some degree, as the archetypal. Indeed, no matter what else the writer may have consciously designed him to be, every storybook hero is likely to be not only archetypal but also charismatic. He is, that is to say, the writer's (local) personification of the hope, such as it is, of mankind. He is in the statistical sense a formulation of that which is a possibility and a probability. He is thus perhaps also a prediction and even a promise, and as such he may be a warning as well as an inspiration. But perhaps an ultimate function is also to make the impossible seem not only possible but imminently (which is to say presently and locally) probable.

Such at any rate is a function of charisma, and such is the basis of the hero's social usefulness. He is man's hope (as the writer finds it to be) of glory, salvation, deliverance, fulfillment, continuity, survival, or even sanity. There is no such thing as a negative hero. Nor can any storybook protagonist be a nonhero. He may be inadequate to his mission, of course, but even so he represents mankind. Not even the meek protagonist in "The Secret Life of Walter Mitty" is a nonhero. His public life is a caricature of suburban conventionality, but his secret life, which represents the most heroic intentions in the world, is the epitome of swashbuckling charisma. Nor, for all their ordinariness, are the actions and achievements of Leopold Bloom in *Ulysses* of a lower order of basic human significance than those of his Homeric prototype.

Nor is there any such thing in literature as a simple story about one individual in one time, place, and circumstance. All stories are examples of some essential aspect of human experience in general, and each is recounted precisely because what it implies has general implications. The unmistakable implication of the traditional narrative expression *Once upon a time* . . . is: "time after time in place after place such and such came to pass." The storyteller fabricates, composes, generalizes, and (if only by implication) moralizes. Human existence, he postulates, is thus and so; for example: time after time there was (and is) a man who, whose circumstances were (and are) such and such, and he did (and does) this and that, and the outcome was and is likely to be as follows. All of which goes to show what human existence is really like. Therefore, human conduct should be like this and not like that. This is good. That is bad. Do this. Avoid that.

Few things are more obvious than the fact that a novel like *Native Son,* for example, was never intended to be read as the simple case history of one atypical U.S. Negro involved in a series of unusual events which relate only to himself. Nor is the *Adventures of Augie March* or *Herzog* the case of one U.S. Jew. Nor is *All the King's Men* that of one or even two white Southerners. *Native Son* is, for all its naturalistic detail, a generalization about Black Americans' behavior as a whole, and it is based on another generalization or assumption about the nature of human nature as a whole: People who are forced to live in subhuman conditions develop sub-human traits; they react subhumanly and become bad people through no fault of their own.

That many do is cause enough for alarm, of course, but the generalization is fallacious and misleading nonetheless. *Most do not!* Many by one means or another maintain a level of conduct which is quite as normal as that of people in normal circumstances —and so achieve another glory for humanity. More-over, not only do others develop above–normal at-tributes, but also much goes to show that the number of people they benefit exceeds to an overwhelming extent the number of those who are damaged or de-stroyed by the others who are reduced to barbarism and diabolical malevolence. One hundred poverty-ridden, oppression–maddened murderers subsisting in the slums of Chicago are certainly more than enough justification for the most urgent rehabilita-tion measures. But in point of actual fact one hun-dred slum–dwelling criminals do not affect as many people as does one single slum–dwelling shoe–shine boy who becomes a doctor, lawyer, preacher, teacher, or even a big league athlete!

The most fundamental as well as the most obvi-ous shortcoming of Bigger Thomas as a symbolic in-dividual U.S. Negro in *Native Son* is that he is an exaggerated oversimplification and is thus an inac-curate statistical projection of both the complexity as well as the potential of Negro life in the United States. He is not even a reliable reflection of the

norms of *abnormal* U.S. Negro behavior. His story
is not a sufficiently representative anecdote about
either Black Americans in particular or about human
nature and conduct in general. It is instead—for all
the literary aspirations which Richard Wright pro-
tests from time to time in "How Bigger was Born"
—mostly only a very special kind of political anecdote. It is an atrocity story, and Wright reveals as
much when he relates that he designed the climax
to register the "moral horror of Negro life in the
United States." Wright also relates that he rejected
the emotional response which his first book, *Uncle
Tom's Children,* evoked from "bankers' daughters,"
and that he was determined to make *Native Son* "so
hard and deep" that people would have to face it
"without the consolation of tears," a statement which
suggests (despite the validity of the intention underlying it) that his own commitment to political action
may have misled him to underestimate the significance of catharsis, in spite of the emphasis which
he placed on the tragic climax.

In any case, *Native Son* is not a tragedy. It is a social science–oriented melodrama with an unhappy
ending. In other words, its plot complications do not
represent the inscrutable "Olympian" contradictions
and humiliations of human existence itself. They re-
flect only the man–made restrictions of an oppres-
sive political system. They do not adequately symbolize the eternal condition of man. They simply
document a very special condition of society and,

what is more, they are predicated on the assumption that such conditions can be ameliorated. Such is the obvious moral of every melodrama; and of course the most insistent if not the only message of revolutionary political and social propaganda is that the dragon must be slain and the curse exorcised so that man can live happily ever afterwards. The moral of tragedy, however, like that of comedy and farce, is that the essential condition of man cannot be ameliorated, but it can be transcended, that struggle is precisely that which gives meaning to movement, that it is in the struggle that one finds one self.

Thus Bigger Thomas is not a tragic hero but rather only a quasi–protagonist who is incapable of performing any of the traditional feats of the melodramatic hero. He does not escape from the dungeon, nor does he rescue the princess and live happily ever afterwards; and instead of removing the menace of the dragon, he himself becomes a villain. He becomes a *natural* product of his environment, only to be destroyed as an "enemy" of society. Such is the extent of Richard Wright's irony, and such is the extent of Bigger Thomas "as a meaningful and prophetic symbol."

But even so, the very title of *Native Son* implies that the story of Bigger Thomas is the representative anecdote about an archetypal Black American. This, of course, is only another way of saying that Richard Wright was no less engaged in an effort to produce

a national epic than were the bards, scops, min-
strels, gleemen, and ballad–makers who created,
danced, and chanted *The Iliad, The Odyssey,* the
Chanson de Roland, the *Nibelungenlied, Beowulf,*
and so on. Nor do the esthetic aspirations behind
the anecdotes of Homer seem to have been more
epical than those behind the song and dance cere-
monies of Hopi, Zuni, and Watusi tribesmen. What
is created, expressed, performed, played, imitated,
reproduced, reenacted, recounted, reflected, and related in each instance is an anecdote which is assumed to represent the essential nature of existence
among a given folk in a given community, commun-
ion of faith, tradition, or nation; hence they are national epics.

PERHAPS such narrative categories as tragedy, comedy, melodrama, and farce may be regarded as specific ritual–statements within the larger ritualistic
framework of the epic. In fact, epic, in its original
sense, was only another word for narration or story-
telling: in this sense, any step or statement that the
aboriginal song and dance man (or maker of *molpês*)
made beyond the simplest, or most impulsive lyric
gesture, as it were, was an epical reenactment. It
was, that is to say, an anecdotal imitation of an
action; and of course as such it required protagonists
and antagonists. These became heroes and obstacles,
and from them came heroic action. Tragedies, come-

dies, melodramas, and farces thus represent special kinds of anecdotes about specific categories of heroic action.

The tragic hero is a representative individual of good intentions or high aspirations who fails because of some fatal flaw within himself and because of the inscrutable ways of nature. The comic hero succeeds to the extent that he learns to live by trial and error. The melodramatic hero proceeds on the assumption that there is a magic key to success! In the narrative category of farce, as construed here, however, the hero survives and succeeds only insofar as he is nimble enough to cope with the slapstick absurdities inherent in the slapdash nature of things.

The slapstick protagonist, like the jam–session soloist, is either nimble or nothing. Moreover, of all the storybook heroes he is perhaps the most comprehensive as well as the most sophisticated archetype of the "successful" individual. Indeed, in a very fundamental sense he seems to begin where all other storybook heroes end. In fact, it is as if he were born with a functional awareness of that which it takes the others a lifetime to learn. His aspirations and intentions are comparable to theirs in every way, but his conception of human nature is significantly different. His definition of integrity, for instance, is much more complicated than that of the tragic hero. Thus he is less vulnerable to the fatal flaw of pride. Somewhat like Jacob in Thomas Mann's *Joseph and His Brothers,* he values his mission, responsibilities, blessings, or long–range aspirations so highly that he can withstand any embarrassment and can even regard humiliation as a passing episode (which incidentally gives him useful information about his adversary's pride).

Unlike the comic protagonist whose adventures are essentially a series of initiation rituals which will enable him to live with the fact that life is one great mystery, the slapstick hero seems to have been oriented to the ambiguities of human experience from the outset. Nor by his standards is the technical skill of the melodramatic hero much more than the beginning of the all–purpose, even if sometimes Chaplinesque, flexibility required by the never-ending ramifications of cosmic slapdash situations.

The adventures of the contemporary detective-story hero are often as melodramatic (or as full of theatrical suspense) as those of the dragon slayers in the old medieval European romances. Nor is this all. The detective, not unlike the noble knight of the quest tradition, is also a man seeking or pursuing something. Furthermore, his success in what he has undertaken to do will result in improved living conditions, an effect which is directly related to the elimination of some menacing element from the landscape. Also, the detective is often depicted as something of a gallant or even as a philanderer, as were some of his medieval forerunners.

But even so, there are differences which are perhaps significant enough to permit a composite of such detectives as Sam Spade, Philip Marlowe, and Dick Tracy to be defined in terms of the context of farce and the blues idiom rather than in that of melodrama, or more specifically, social science fiction fiction—which is to say Marx–Freud heroism. To begin with, the detective–story hero is in quest not of the Holy Grail and salvation, but of evidence concerning the source or sources of "evil." Indeed, for all the fisticuffs and shoot–em–ups so frequently involved, the detective–story hero's quest may perhaps be more appropriately described as a research mission. As a matter of fact, the detective, as his very name suggests, is in actuality a research technician above all else. Unlike the social science fiction fiction research hero, however, who is very likely to be a Marxian–Freudian deliverer discovering or inventing some all–purpose device or magic cure, the detective is mostly concerned with clues bearing on the nature and cause of specific troubles. He regards technological devices as useful gadgets, but he is not so naïve as to expect human nature to be made any less human by them.

The obvious fact is that the detective functions in terms of a conception of science and of what scientific method and insight can and cannot accomplish that is more sophisticated than that of the Marx–Freud Knight–Errant. He employs scientific procedure with the consummate expertise of, say, the most advanced physicists. But behold, he also follows tips, plays hunches, buys scraps of data from informers or stool pigeons; and he eavesdrops as a matter of course. He is, in other words, a researcher whose openmindedness is closely geared to precisely the sort of riff-style improvisation that typifies the blues idiom sensibility.

And finally, when the contemporary detective achieves his stated objective, he has done only that, as it were. It is not assumed that his successful action has rid the environment of any such all-powerful dragons or curses as were drying up all streams and turning the whole countryside into a wasteland. He has exposed one or maybe several sources of social misfortune. But there is always another and another no less urgent assignment awaiting his return to the office. In the detective story the hero seldom gets but the briefest respite between clients and cases. He is forever being called away from his hobby, a vacation, the racetrack, or the arms of some marvelously intriguing woman because the times are out of joint once again.

In still other words, then, the detective-story hero may also be classified as a species of blues idiom hero, a *nada*-confrontation hero, which is also to say, a slapstick hero, not only because of the nature of his quest and certain characteristics of his sensibility, but also because his behavior is so compatible with his circumstances, which are nothing if not slapdash jam-session situation or predicament in the first place.

As much as has been made of the literary implica-

tions of existentialism, little if any attention seems to
have been given to the comprehensive significance
of farce and the slapstick hero. But then perhaps the
so–called nonhero of recent avant–garde fiction (or
is it avant–garde commentary?) represents an effort
to describe a protagonist for cosmic slapstick situations. If so, the results leave much to be desired as
an archetypal image of the contemporary individual in the United States. The so–called nonhero,
after all, is not only unable to achieve any functional equilibrium in terms of the blues tradition of
antagonistic cooperation; he is, alas, only a sad sack
of a man for whom all situations are overwhelming. Thus where the blues–oriented slapstick or jam–
session hero is ever alert and agile, as only befits
one whom U.S. transportation and communication
facilities have made heir to all times and places, the
so–called nonhero is either a benumbed victim of
circumstances or an anxious alien. (Even where he
occupies the official seat of all but limitless power,
he is likely to proceed as if he were an innocent
stranger who has somehow or other been unjustly
condemned, completely forgetting, as the blues–
oriented hero would not, that guilt is inherent in
man's humanity and that heroes often increase their
guilt in the very process of performing good deeds!)

And yet the dynamics of farce and cosmic slapstick heroism seem to underlie much if not most of
the literature of Europe and America. The gods on
Mount Olympus, for example, to whom thunderbolt

slinging and the manipulation of storm winds and tidal waves were no more serious than vaudevillian pie throwing, obviously regarded human existence as a farce. To them, according to the writers who depicted them, the confusions and insecurities of the ancient Greek mortals were all too often only a matter of capricious concern at best. It was not for nothing that the wily Odysseus was a picaresque hero whose nimbleness was his fortune. Nor has his survival as an archetype been inconsistent with the fundamental European conception of human actuality.

But perhaps even more curious is the fact that most contemporary U.S. intellectuals have made next to nothing of the inevitable connection between existential absurdity and the concept of antagonistic cooperation. All the same, there is no narrative tradition which is more fundamental to European and American literature. Nor is any conception of human endeavor more inherently ludicrous. It is sheer nonsense to insist that obstacles are really opportunities and that chaos is constructive! Nevertheless, most stories are irrefutable evidence that such is precisely the urgent secret which most of the great masters of fiction have always been trying to reveal.

No less obvious are the images of the world as farce in the work of such masters of contemporary fiction as André Malraux, Thomas Mann, and Ernest Hemingway. The human condition as described by Malraux is utterly absurd. For the Malraux protagonist, however, it is as if such absurdities as chaos, nature-in-the-raw, fate, and the inscrutable were simply other terms for dragon, which of course is only a romantic synonym for *requirement for hero-ism*. Indeed, the fiction of Malraux, far from being non-heroic, represents the world of the composite epic hero. Essentially all of Malraux's stories are anecdotes about contemporary men who are involved with primordial issues. Such, according to *The Voices of Silence*, is man's fate, but perhaps that which defines man's fate also suggests man's hope.

When in *Attitudes Toward History*, Kenneth Burke speaking of what he calls poetic categories classifies the epic (as well as the tragic and comic) in terms of a frame of acceptance (as opposed to such frames of rejection as plaints, elegies, satires, etc.) he is not talking about accepting one's sorry lot in some god-awful socio-political structure or of making one's peace with the devil. What Burke describes as a fundamental function of the epic as a poetic category can also be applied to farce as defined here, and also to the blues idiom. Indeed the blues statement is nothing if not an experience-confrontation device that enables people to begin by accepting the difficult, disappointing, chaotic, absurd, which is to say the farcical or existential facts of life. Moreover, even as it does so it also prepares or disposes people to accept the necessity for struggle.

The Joseph story of Thomas Mann is a definitive representation of the world as farce (and of man as quick–witted, nimble–footed dreamer in action). There is, to begin with, the all–inclusive absurdity inherent in the relativity of time, which is at once the container of consciousness and that which consciousness contains, the all and the nothingness of past–present–future am—isness. Then there is Jacob the hoaxer, son of Isaac; Jacob who hoaxes Esau—to get that which was already his by birthright—only to be hoaxed by Laban, by Joseph, and by The Brothers (at the time of Joseph's disappearance). Jacob's dearest bliss, like his deepest despair, is the response to a hoax.

There is also Joseph himself, whose completely fantastic career, as Thomas Mann recounts it, is one long chronicle of metaphysical dreams which become political schemes. But after all, Joseph, whose misfortune—for much of which he is personally responsible—is outrageously interwoven with his good luck, is only an extension and elaboration of the preposterous but altogether fascinating notion that Jacob was as much concerned with creating God as with serving Him. In Joseph as in Jacob, both past masters of the lunar syntax of artful fabrication, Mann has embodied yet another prototype of the contemporary writer as one whose special insight into the mysterious interrelationship of illusion and reality is as much a burden as it is a blessing.

Nothing is more curious, more challenging, or,

upon reflection, more platitudinous than the assumption of Jacob and of Joseph that experience is for the most part what you are able to make it. Nor is any notion more implicitly existential or fundamental to the cosmos of Hemingway, all of the values of which were conceived (made–up, not described) in full, clear, well–lighted cognizance of the innate absurdity of all–enveloping *nada*. No hero in contemporary fiction is more acutely aware of the vanity of human wishes and endeavors than is Frederick Henry in *A Farewell to Arms;* and certainly no one, not even K, the completely lost and confused land surveyor (!) in Kafka's *The Castle,* knows better than Jake Barnes in *The Sun Also Rises* that deadpan slapstick is slapstick nonetheless. But then, as so much of his fiction suggests, Ernest Hemingway, whose response mechanisms were as sensitive to the textures of existence in the United States as to those of the contemporary world at large, was essentially a maker of blues ballad extensions.

So much is obvious if only by inference, and in addition much goes to show that the blues tradition itself is, among other things, an extension of the old American frontier tradition (which, incidentally, was always as applicable to the city and the plantation as to the wilderness, the mountains, and the plains). There is, for instance, the same seemingly inherent emphasis on rugged individual endurance. There is also the candid acknowledgment and sober acceptance of adversity as an inescapable condition of human existence—and perhaps in consequence an affirmative disposition toward all obstacles, whether urban or rural, whether political or metaphysical. In all events, the slapstick situation is the natural habitat of the blues–oriented hero—who qualifies as a frontiersman in the final analysis if only because he is a man who expects the best but is always prepared, at least emotionally when not otherwise, for the worst.

But perhaps above all else the blues–oriented hero image represents the American embodiment of the man whose concept of being able to live happily ever afterwards is most consistent with the moral of all dragon–encounters: *Improvisation is the ultimate human* (i.e., *heroic*) *endowment.* It is, indeed; and even as flexibility or the ability to swing (or to perform with grace under pressure) is the key to that unique competence which generates the self–reliance and thus the charisma of the hero, and even as infinite alertness–become–dexterity is the functional source of the magic of all master craftsmen, so may skill in the art of improvisation be that which both will enable contemporary man to be at home with his sometimes tolerable but never quite certain condition of *not* being at home in the world and will also dispose him to regard his obstacles and frustrations as well as his achievements in terms of adventure and romance.

The Seven League Boots

A NOVEL

by Albert Murray

By an American master, "a fictional tale spinner in the grand Southern tradition" (*Washington Post Book World*), *The Seven League Boots* tells the story of Scooter, a recent graduate from an Alabama college in the 1920s who is hired as a temporary bass player in the traveling band of the legendary jazz musician and composer the Bossman (the "Emperor of Syncopation"). As Bossman and the band chart new territory, the tour becomes a heroic journey—"equivalent to the seven league stride of the heroes in rocking chair story times"—retracing Sherman's march to the sea, the Underground Railroad, the Great Migration, the Gold Rush, and the conquest of the West. Lyrical and engaging, *The Seven League Boots* brilliantly dramatizes what it means for a black man to fulfill the "ancestral imperative": to survive and thrive through improvisation and style.

FICTION/LITERATURE/0-679-75858-5

Printed in the United States
by Baker & Taylor Publisher Services